A FIRST BOOK FOR UNDERSTANDING DIABETES

This book is a synopsis of the larger book, _Understanding Diabetes_.
It provides a quick summary of each of the 28 chapters.
It may be easier to begin learning from this book until people are ready
to read the larger book.

i

This book is dedicated to Alice Green in appreciation for trying to keep me "organized" (sometimes).

SPECIAL THANKS TO...

- The staff of the Children's Diabetes Foundation and The Guild of the Children's Diabetes Foundation at Denver.

- Sherrie Harris, BSN, MA, CDE and Regina Reece for editing, proofreading, and manuscript preparation.

- Cindy Barton for book design, graphics, and illustrations.

- MGM Consumer Products for allowing the use of The Pink Panther™ & ©2004 UNITED ARTISTS CORPORATION. All rights reserved. www.pinkpanther.com

- Additional copies of this publication may be purchased from The Guild of the Children's Diabetes Foundation at Denver. See available publications on the last page of this book.

TABLE OF CONTENTS

The chapters in this book follow the chapters in _Understanding Diabetes_, 10th edition.

Chapter 1 THE IMPORTANCE OF EDUCATION IN DIABETES

It is important to learn all about diabetes. At the time of diagnosis, the family will spend two to three days learning about diabetes. A week later they will return for another day. This book will help in the beginning, until the family is ready to read _Understanding Diabetes_. In both books, the chapters have the same numbers and topics. All family members, including both parents, should be present for initial education.

🐾 The **first** day of teaching often includes:

❑ What diabetes is and what causes it
❑ Urine and/or blood ketone testing
❑ Blood sugar testing
❑ Recognizing a low blood sugar and how to treat it

❑ Insulin types and actions
❑ Drawing up insulin
❑ Giving insulin shots
❑ Food survival skills

🐾 On the **second** day, the topics from day one are reviewed and a family member gives the shot. Other areas often covered are:

❑ A school plan
❑ Directions for diabetes care using the telephone
❑ Details of treatment (including "thinking" scales)

❑ Education about food (dietitian)
❑ Feelings (psych-social team)
❑ Plans for the next few days

The **one week** visit is usually all day and includes a group presentation from the nutritionist as well as a review of insulin activity, treating low and high blood sugars, checking ketones and when to contact the diabetes care providers.

In addition, the importance of the hemoglobin A_{1c} test, of recording blood sugars and looking at patterns, proper sick-day management, ketoacidosis (DKA) and the honeymoon period are all discussed. An individualized clinic visit occurs in the afternoon.

The importance of education in diabetes.

Special instructions for the first night are:

New Patient First-Night Instructions for _____

A. **The diabetes supplies you will need the first night include** (your nurse will mark which you need):

____ Blood glucose meter ____ Meter test strips ____ Alcohol swabs
____ Ketone check strips ____ Glucose gel & tabs ____ Log book
____ Insulin ____ Syringes ____ Phone contact card

The first night you will either get your insulin injection at our clinic, or you will give the shot at home or where you are staying.

B. *If the insulin is given while at the clinic:*

❑ 1. Humalog®/NovoLog® insulin has been given; eat within 10-15 minutes.

❑ 2. Regular insulin has been given, try to eat your meal within 30 minutes – or – have a snack containing carbohydrates on the way home if it will be more than 30 minutes.

3. Allow your child to eat until their appetite is satisfied, avoiding high sugar foods (especially regular sugar pop and sweet desserts).

C. *If the dinner insulin is to be given at home:*

1. Check your child's blood sugar right before your meal. Enter the result into the log book.

2. Check for urine ketones. Enter the result into the log book.

3. Call Dr. _____ at _____ or page at _____ for an insulin dose.
    Give this dose: _____.

4. Draw up and give the insulin injection right before your meal (see Chapter 8). If your child is not very hungry or is tired, you can give the shot after they eat and call the physician with any dose questions.

5. Eat your meal, allowing your child to eat until their appetite is satisfied. Avoid high sugar foods.

D. *Before Bed:*

1. Check your child's blood sugar. Enter the result into the log book.

2. Check for urine ketones. Enter the result into the log book.

3. Call your physician at the numbers listed above if your child's blood sugar is below ____ or above ____, or if urine ketones are "moderate" or "large". If urine ketones are "trace" or "small", have your child drink 8-12 oz of water before going to bed.

4. Give an insulin injection if your physician instructs you to do so. (Dose, if ordered _____.)

5. Have your child eat a bedtime snack. Some ideas for this snack include: cereal and milk, toast and peanut butter, a slice of pizza, yogurt and graham crackers or cheese and crackers. (See Chapter 11, Table 2 in the *Understanding Diabetes* book for other ideas.)

E. *The second morning before coming to the clinic:*

1. If your physician has instructed you to give the morning insulin at home before coming in, follow the steps listed above (see letter "C") for last night's meal dose **before** eating breakfast.

2. If you have been instructed to wait to give the morning dose until after coming to the clinic, do a blood sugar test and a urine ketone test upon awakening (if blood sugar is less than 70, give 4–6 oz of juice promptly).

    Write the blood sugar and urine ketone results in your log book.
    ❑ Eat breakfast at home, and then come to the clinic for your insulin injection.
    ❑ Bring your breakfast to the clinic, and you will eat it after the insulin has been given.

3. Please bring all blood testing supplies and materials you received the first day back to the clinic (including your log book, Pink Panther book, insulin and supplies).

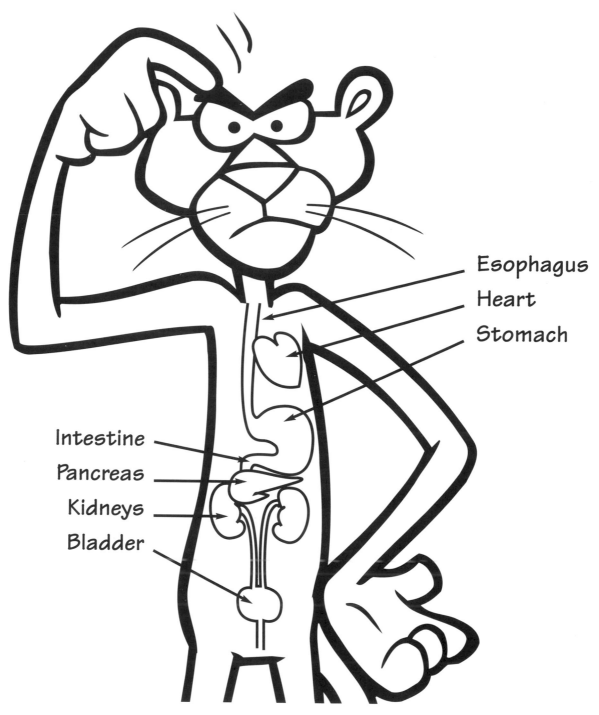

Esophagus

Heart

Stomach

Intestine

Pancreas

Kidneys

Bladder

Insulin is made in the body by an organ called the pancreas. The difference between people with type 1 diabetes and people with type 2 diabetes is the pancreas of a person with type 1 diabetes stops making enough insulin.

In type 2 diabetes, the pancreas can still make insulin, but the insulin does not work like it should.

Chapter 2: WHAT IS DIABETES?

Type 1 (Childhood, Juvenile, Insulin-dependent) **diabetes** is due to not enough insulin being made in the pancreas (see picture). The most common signs are:

🐾 **frequent passing of urine**

🐾 **constant thirst**

🐾 **weight loss**

For people with **type 1 diabetes**, insulin must be taken through a needle. Insulin cannot be taken as a pill because the stomach acid would destroy it.

Type 1 diabetes is different from **type 2 diabetes** (adult-onset, or non-insulin dependent diabetes) where insulin is still made but doesn't work very well. People with type 2 diabetes can sometimes use pills (which are not insulin) and diet and exercise to control their diabetes (see Chapter 4). Eating healthy food and exercising are also important for people with type 1 diabetes, but they will always need to take insulin shots.

Insulin allows sugar to pass into our cells to be used for energy. It also turns off the body's making of sugar. When not enough insulin is present, the sugar cannot pass into the body's cells. The sugar is high in the blood and it passes out in the urine. Frequent passing of urine is the result. (See Figures on the next 2 pages.)

Because sugar cannot be used for energy, the body breaks down fat for energy. Ketones are the result of using fat for energy.

When insulin treatment begins, the urine ketones (see Chapter 5) gradually disappear. After a few days, the blood sugars become lower and the passing of urine and drinking of water will be less often. Weight is gained back and the person starts to feel much better.

Often a **"honeymoon"** time begins a few weeks or months after a person with type 1 diabetes starts insulin shots. The insulin dose (amount of insulin given) may go down and it may seem like the person does not have diabetes, but **THEY DO!** This period may last from two weeks to two years.

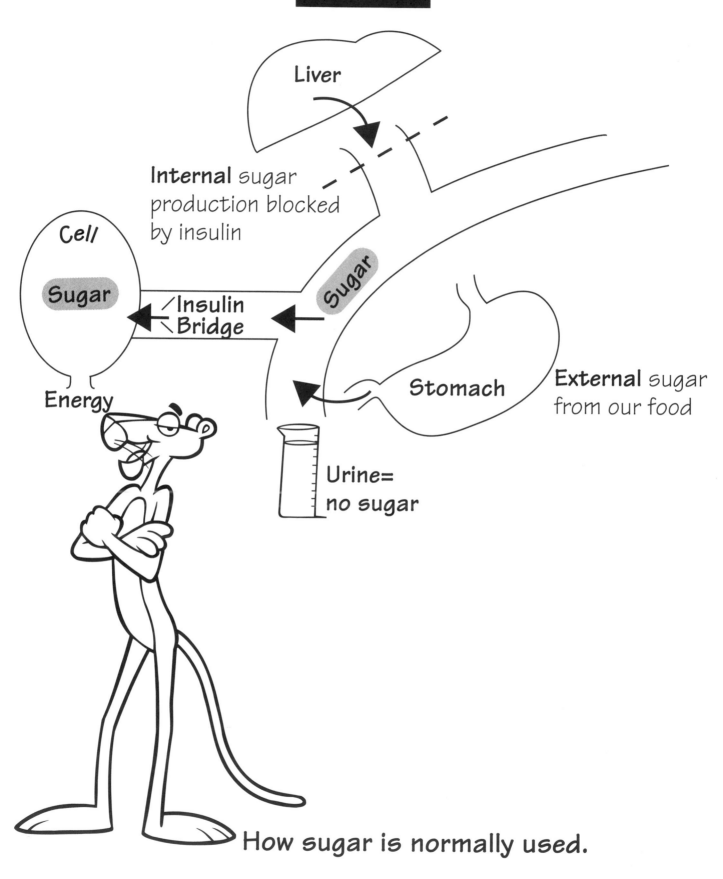

NORMAL

Liver

Internal sugar production blocked by insulin

Cell

Sugar

Energy

Insulin Bridge

Sugar

Stomach

External sugar from our food

Urine= no sugar

How sugar is normally used.

DIABETES

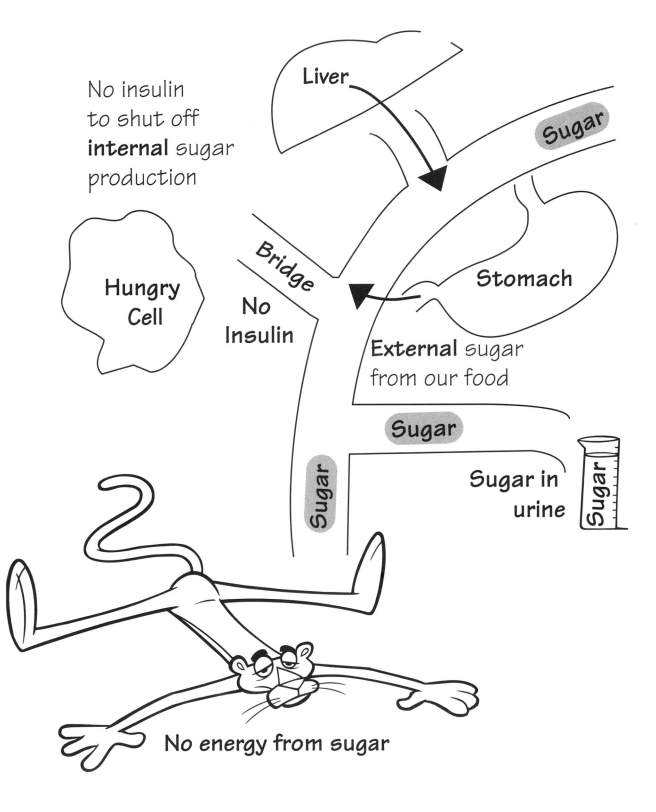

No insulin to shut off **internal** sugar production

Liver

Sugar

Hungry Cell

Bridge

No Insulin

Stomach

External sugar from our food

Sugar

Sugar

Sugar in urine

Sugar

No energy from sugar

What happens to sugar in a person with diabetes.

The mystery of what causes type 1 diabetes is now better understood.

Chapter 3   WHAT CAUSES TYPE 1 DIABETES?

The cause of type 1 diabetes is believed to be due to three things:

❶ Genetics: Genes come from both mom and dad and can make someone more likely to get diabetes. Over half of the people that get type 1 diabetes have inherited the gene cell types DR3/DR4. (One is from mom and one is from dad.)

❷ Self-Allergy (autoimmunity):

• The immune system in the body normally protects it from possible harm.

• An allergy is a reaction by the body's immune system to something it thinks doesn't belong inside the body.

• Self-allergy is when a person's body develops an allergy against one of its own parts. In this case, the allergy is against the islet (eye-let) cells in the pancreas where insulin is made. When the islet cells have been damaged, the immune system makes something called antibodies. These antibodies are present in the blood (**I**slet **C**ell **A**ntibodies or **ICA**).

Other antibodies which may be found in the blood of people with type 1 diabetes are:

• IAA (insulin autoantibody)

• GAD antibody

• ICA-512 antibody

Sometimes these antibodies are present for many years before the signs of diabetes appear. Half of the people who will someday develop type 1 diabetes already have the antibodies by age five years. Being able to identify antibodies has allowed studies (which have begun in the U.S. and Europe) to try to prevent type 1 diabetes (see Chapter 28 on Research).

❸ Virus or Chemical: Having a certain gene makeup may allow a virus or chemical to get to the islet cells (where insulin is made) and cause damage. Once the damage has occurred, the self-allergy likely begins.

TYPE 2 DIABETES

Type 2 (adult-onset) diabetes does not occur as a result of the self-allergy like type 1 diabetes. Therefore, antibodies (found in type 1 diabetes) are not present in the blood.

Type 2 has an inherited part (Chapter 4), but the genetics are different from type 1 diabetes. As noted in Chapter 2, people with type 2 diabetes may have normal or high insulin levels. The insulin just does not work well. In contrast, people with type 1 diabetes have low or no insulin. The two conditions are both called diabetes. Both result in high sugars, but they are VERY different from each other.

Thirty minutes of exercise five times a week is important for people with type 2 diabetes.

Chapter 4

TYPE 2 DIABETES (NON-INSULIN DEPENDENT DIABETES MELLITUS [NIDDM])

Type 2 diabetes is the most common type to occur in adults over age 40 years. It is quite common in Native-Americans. Also, at least half of African-American and Hispanic youth with diabetes have type 2 diabetes.

CAUSE

Type 2 diabetes is partly **inherited (genetic)**. It is also linked with being overweight and not getting enough exercise. It is often called a "**disease of life-styles.**" Our ancestors were very active and ate less. We now live in a world of automobile travel, television, computers, video games and high calorie fast foods.

SYMPTOMS

The symptoms can be the same as with type 1 diabetes (Chapter 2). They may be:

- frequent drinking of liquids
- frequent urination (going to the bathroom)
- infections
- sores which heal slowly
- no energy
- Many people don't have any symptoms. These people are sometimes diagnosed by a high blood sugar that is measured on a routine physical exam. Others are diagnosed when they have a high blood sugar level on a test called an Oral Glucose Tolerance Test.

TREATMENT: Changes in lifestyle are <u>very important</u>.

• Eating foods with fewer calories and carbohydrates as well as less fat is needed.

• Getting at least 30 minutes of exercise five to seven days a week is very important.

• Checking blood sugars (like people with type 1 diabetes) is helpful (Chapter 7). The blood sugar values can tell you how you are doing each day.

• If at diagnosis a person has ketones, insulin shots are usually needed. The shots are needed during times of illness.

• Medications by mouth can be tried if the blood sugars and HbA$_{1c}$ (Chapter 14) return to near normal. Often by losing weight and exercising, blood sugars will return to near normal.

• These medicines taken by mouth ARE NOT insulin. When taken, these medicines cause the pancreas to make more insulin. They can also make the body more sensitive to its own insulin.

One of these medicines is called *Glucophage®* (metformin).

• This medicine is usually tried first.

• Sometimes it can cause an upset stomach.

• If a person becomes sick, this medicine must be stopped until they are well. It can cause a condition called lactic acidosis. Insulin shots may be needed during the illness. Call your doctor or nurse if you are not sure what to do.

• There are other medicines taken by mouth that can be tried if Glucophage causes too much stomach upset or isn't working well.

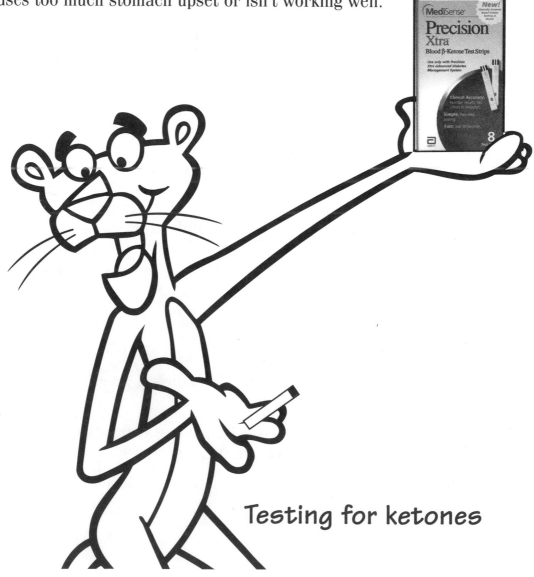

Testing for ketones

Chapter KETONE TESTING

Ketone testing is very easy and very important.

A. NEWLY DIAGNOSED PERSON:

The first goal for new patients is to clear their ketones.

Ketones come from fat breakdown. Insulin stops fat breakdown and prevents ketones from being made.

The second goal is to lower their blood sugar levels.

Insulin also turns off sugar production from the liver.

B. A PERSON WITH KNOWN DIABETES:

When to check for ketones (either in urine or blood):

• during any illness

• with a very high blood sugar (e.g.: above 300 mg/dl [16.7 mmol/L])

• if an insulin shot is missed

• after vomiting even once

• with a blockage of an insulin pump catheter or pump failure

If ketones are present, extra insulin can be given to stop the ketones from being made. (Ketones need to be found early and extra insulin given or the person may get very sick; see Chapter 15.)

C. HOW TO TEST FOR KETONES

A method to test for ketones must always be in the home and taken along on trips. Failure to do the ketone test when indicated could result in the person becoming very sick. Ketones can be checked using either urine or a drop of blood. The urine test is cheaper, although testing the blood has the advantage of telling how high the ketones are at that moment (as well as other advantages).

URINE TESTING

The two main strips used are:

1. Ketostix®: comes in foil wrapping that allows them to last longer.

This strip is dipped into the urine and is read as negative, trace, small, moderate, large, or large-large after *exactly* 15 seconds.

2. Chemstrip K®: comes in bottles and are not foil wrapped. All non-foil wrapped strips (including non-foil wrapped Ketostix in a bottle) must be thrown out six months after the bottle is opened.

This strip is dipped into the urine and is read as negative, trace, small, moderate, large or large-large after *exactly* 60 seconds.

BLOOD TESTING

Some people prefer to use the Precision Xtra® meter to test blood ketones.

• The red calibration strip must be placed in the meter first.

• Next the blood ketone strip is inserted with the three black bars facing up.

• Then a drop of blood is placed in the purple hole of the strip.

• The result is given in 30 seconds.

Table 1. COMPARISON OF BLOOD AND URINE KETONE READINGS

Blood Ketone (mmol/L)	Urine Ketone Strip color	Level	Action to take
less than 0.6	slight/no color change	negative	normal - no action needed
0.6 to 1.5	light purple	small to moderate**	extra insulin & fluids***
1.6 to 3.0	dark purple	usually large	call MD or RN**
greater than 3.0	very dark purple	very large	**go directly to the E.R.**

It is usually advised to call a health care provider for a blood ketone level greater than 1.5 or with urine ketone readings of moderate or large.

If the blood glucose level is below 150 mg/dl (8.3 mmol/L), a liquid with glucose should be taken.

Chapter 6

LOW BLOOD SUGAR (HYPOGLYCEMIA or INSULIN REACTION)

Anyone who has been given insulin can have low blood sugar (hypoglycemia or a "reaction"). **A true low blood sugar is a value less than 60 mg/dl (3.2 mmol/L).**

Main Causes:

- late or missed meals or snacks
- extra exercise
- too much insulin/wrong dose
- taking bath, shower or hot tub too soon after injection
- low blood sugar (for any reason, particularly at bedtime) and failing to do a follow-up blood sugar 15 to 30 minutes later, making sure the value has come up as a result of the treatment
- illnesses with vomiting

Remember that if a person has a low blood sugar and can't keep food down, low dose glucagon, one unit per year of age up to 18 units, can be given under the skin just like insulin - with an insulin syringe. The dose can be repeated every 20 minutes until the blood sugar is up.

The signs of a low blood sugar can be different and may include:

- hunger
- feeling shaky, sweaty and/or weak
- confusion
- sleepiness (at unusual times)
- behavioral/mood changes
- double vision
- the signs of nighttime lows may be the same, or may include waking up alert, crying or having bad dreams

Low blood sugar comes on quickly. It must be treated immediately by the person (if able) or by someone who is nearby at the time. If not treated, loss of consciousness or seizures may occur. Different levels of reactions (mild, moderate, severe) and treatment for each level are shown in the table in this chapter.

With a "mild" low blood sugar: (also see table)

• give sugar (it's best in liquid form) such as four ounces of juice or sugar pop or eight ounces of milk.

• when possible, a blood sugar test should be done.

• it takes **10 to 20 minutes** for the blood sugar to rise after treatment.

• re-check the blood sugar after 10 to 20 minutes to make sure the level is above 70 mg/dl (3.9 mmol/L).

• if it is still below this level, the liquid sugar should be given again. Follow the steps above, again.

• wait another 10 to 15 minutes to repeat the blood sugar test.

• if the blood sugar is above 70 mg/dl (3.9 mmol/L), give solid food. The reason for waiting to give the solid food is that it may soak up the liquid sugar and slow the time for the sugar to get into the blood.

• the person should not return to activity until the blood sugar is above 70 mg/dl (3.9 mmol/L).

• if the low is at bedtime, it is best to repeat the blood sugar test during the night to make sure the level stays up.

• if a low blood sugar occurs when it is time for an insulin shot, always treat the low first. Make sure the blood sugar is back up before giving the shot.

With a "moderate" or "severe" reaction:

• put half a tube of Insta-Glucose® or cake gel between the gums and cheeks. Rub the cheeks and stroke the throat to help with swallowing.

• if a seizure or complete loss of consciousness occurs, it may be necessary to give a shot of **glucagon**.

Though the result of using glucagon is the opposite of insulin, it is <u>NOT</u> sugar. It will make the blood sugar rise, usually in **10 to 20 minutes**.

Giving glucagon:

🐾 after mixing, it can be given with an insulin syringe just like insulin.

Amount of glucagon to give:

🐾 preschoolers can be given a full 30 unit syringe.

🐾 preteens can be given a full 50 unit syringe.

🐾 teens and adults can be given a full 100 unit syringe.

🐾 if the person does not respond in 10 to 20 minutes, the paramedics (911) should be called.

Your doctor or nurse should be called prior to the next insulin shot, as the amount of insulin you give may need to be changed.

Never give a shot and then get in a shower, bathtub or hot tub. The blood coming to the skin surface may cause the insulin to be rapidly absorbed. This may result in a severe insulin reaction.

HYPOGLYCEMIA: Treatment of Low Blood Sugar (B.S.)

Always check blood sugar level!

Low Blood Sugar Category	MILD	MODERATE	SEVERE
Alertness	Alert	*NOT* Alert Unable to drink safely (choking risk) Needs help from another person	*Unresponsive* Loss of consciousness Seizure **Needs constant adult help** ***Give nothing by mouth*** (extreme choking risk)
Symptoms	Mood changes Shaky, sweaty Hungry Fatigue, weak Pale	Lack focus Confused Disoriented 'Out of control' (biting, kicking) ***Can't*** self-treat	Loss of consciousness Seizure
Actions to Take	Check blood sugar (B.S.). Give 3 oz sugary fluid (amount age dependent) Recheck B.S. in 10-20 min. B.S. less than 70, repeat sugary fluid and recheck in 10-20 min. B.S. greater than 70, give a solid snack	Check B.S. Give Insta-Glucose® or Cake Mate® put between gums and teeth and rub in Look for person to 'wake up' **Once alert** - follow "actions" under '**MILD**' COLUMN	***Place in position of safety*** Check B.S. Glucagon: *can be given with an insulin syringe* like insulin Recheck B.S. in 10-20 min Below 5 years : **30 units** 5-18 years: **50 units** Over 18 years: **100 units (all of dose)** **Check B.S. every 10-20 min. until greater than 70** **Check B.S. every hour x 4-5 hours** If no response, may need to call 911 High risk for more lows x 24 hours (need to ↑ food intake & ↓ insulin doses)
Recovery Time	10-20 minutes	20-45 minutes	**Call RN / MD and report the episode** (effects can last 2-12 hours)

18

It is important for adults to keep an eye on younger children for signs of low sugar.

Test your blood sugars four or more times each day.

Chapter 7

BLOOD SUGAR (GLUCOSE) TESTING

WHEN?

- ❤ four or more times each day (usually before meals and the bedtime snack)
- ❤ food should not be eaten within the two hours before a test
- ❤ anytime the symptoms of a low blood sugar are felt
- ❤ once weekly, two hours after each meal
- ❤ occasionally during the night

BLOOD SUGAR LEVELS

A normal blood sugar (when no food has been eaten for two or more hours) is 70-120 mg/dl (3.9-6.6 mmol/L)*.

Symptoms

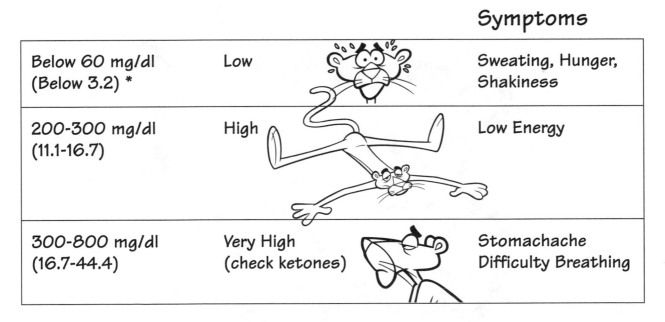

			Symptoms
Below 60 mg/dl (Below 3.2) *	Low		Sweating, Hunger, Shakiness
200-300 mg/dl (11.1-16.7)	High		Low Energy
300-800 mg/dl (16.7-44.4)	Very High (check ketones)		Stomachache Difficulty Breathing

GOALS

The values for which to aim are different for each age group and are shown in the table below. At least half of the values at each time of day should be in the desired range for age. The values refer both to fasting and anytime food has not been eaten for two or more hours.

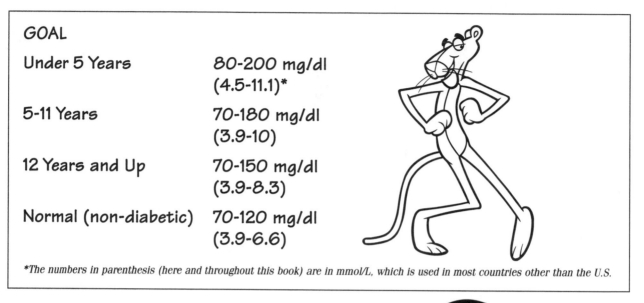

GOAL

Under 5 Years	80-200 mg/dl (4.5-11.1)*
5-11 Years	70-180 mg/dl (3.9-10)
12 Years and Up	70-150 mg/dl (3.9-8.3)
Normal (non-diabetic)	70-120 mg/dl (3.9-6.6)

The numbers in parenthesis (here and throughout this book) are in mmol/L, which is used in most countries other than the U.S.

DOING THE TESTING

Finger-Pokes: There are now many good devices. Most can be set for different depths. These may help young children or the elderly who do not need a lancet to go as deep.

How to:

🐾 Get poker ready; insert lancet (change daily).

🐾 Wash hands with soap and warm water; dry.

🐾 Poke side or tip (not ball) of chosen finger or of arm (alternate site testing)**.

🐾 To get enough blood, hold hand down (below heart level) and "milk" the finger.

🐾 Wipe off the first drop of blood with a cotton ball.

🐾 Put the second drop of blood on the test strip as taught for each meter.

🐾 Hold cotton ball on poke site to stop bleeding.

Meters: We do not recommend one meter over another.

• We do like meters that can store at least the last 100 values.

• The meter must also be able to be downloaded by the family or clinic.

• Strips requiring smaller amounts of blood make it easier for young children.

• Make sure the code in the meter matches the code for the strips.

• **The meter must always be brought to the clinic visit.**

**Alternate Site Testing: Some meters now require such a small drop of blood that it can be obtained from the arm or another site.

**However, *if feeling low, the fingertip must be used* as circulation is not as good in other sites and the true blood sugar level may be delayed by 10-20 minutes.

Log books: It is important to record results.

• Look for patterns of highs and lows.

• If too many lows occur, the results should be sent to the nurse or doctor by fax or e-mail (e.g., more than 2 values per week below 60 mg/dl [3.2 mmol/L]).

• If too many highs occur, the results should be sent to the nurse or doctor by fax or e-mail, (e.g., more than 2 values at the same time of day in a week above 300 mg/dl [16.7 mmol/L]).

• Parents (even of teens) must do or supervise the recording of the values and the sending of the results.

• **Bring the log book to the clinic visit.**

Psyche: It is important not to be upset if highs or lows are found. This can make testing a negative experience. Just use the data to adjust the insulin and/or to prevent future highs or lows. The only response should be "**Thank you for doing the test.**"

Stay calm, the blood sugar will *come* down.

Chapter 8

INSULIN: TYPES AND ACTIVITY

WHY ARE INSULIN SHOTS NEEDED?

- Not enough insulin is made in the pancreas of a person with type 1 diabetes.

- Insulin can't be taken as a pill because it would be destroyed by stomach acid.

- People with type 2 diabetes who have ketones or very high blood sugars also usually take insulin shots, at least in the beginning.

THE THREE TYPES OF INSULIN ARE:

1. *"short-acting"* (Humalog, NovoLog and Regular)

    • Humalog and NovoLog are more rapid-acting than Regular; they peak earlier and do not last as long as Regular insulin.

    • Humalog, NovoLog and Regular insulins are clear.

2. *"intermediate-acting"* (NPH, Lente®, Ultralente®)

    • Most intermediate-acting insulins are cloudy and must be mixed to get the same dose with each shot.

    • The bottles should be turned up and down 20 times before drawing the insulin into the syringe.

    • The NPH, Lente and Ultralente insulins peak during the day when food is being eaten.

3. *"long-acting"* (Lantus® or insulin glargine; see table)

    • It is the first true basal (flat-acting, no peak) insulin that lasts 24 hours.

    • It is a <u>clear</u> insulin.

    • It must be drawn into the syringe alone (cannot be mixed with any other insulin).

** Insulin must be stored so that it does not freeze or get over 90° F because it will spoil. **

HOW AND WHEN IS INSULIN USED?

Most people take two or more shots of insulin each day.

SHORT-ACTING INSULIN USES:

* Short-acting insulins are used to stop the rise of the blood sugar after eating food.

* The short-acting insulin can be mixed with the intermediate-acting insulin to give before breakfast and dinner.

* If Humalog or NovoLog is used, it should be taken just before the meal.

* If Regular insulin is being used, the shot is usually taken 30 minutes before meals.

* For toddlers: Humalog or NovoLog can be given after the meal. Then the dose can be adjusted to fit the amount of food eaten.

* Some people also take a shot of short-acting insulin at lunch or at the time of the afternoon snack.

* Short-acting insulins are also used to "correct" a blood sugar level that is too high (see Correction Insulin Dose: Chapter 21).

Figure 1: Two Shots Per Day

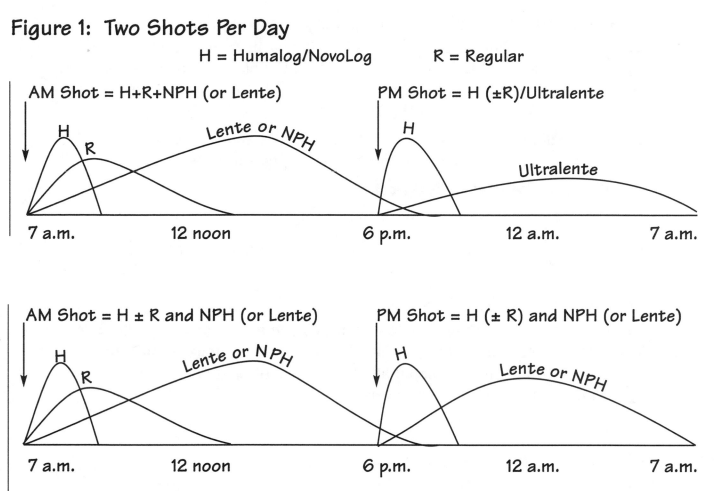

H = Humalog/NovoLog   R = Regular

AM Shot = H+R+NPH (or Lente)   PM Shot = H (±R)/Ultralente

H R   Lente or NPH   H   Ultralente

7 a.m.   12 noon   6 p.m.   12 a.m.   7 a.m.

AM Shot = H ± R and NPH (or Lente)   PM Shot = H (± R) and NPH (or Lente)

H R   Lente or NPH   H   Lente or NPH

7 a.m.   12 noon   6 p.m.   12 a.m.   7 a.m.

Many people receive two injections per day of NPH or Lente as their intermediate-acting insulin. They can then take Humalog/NovoLog or Regular or both with the NPH or Lente (see figure above).

INTERMEDIATE-ACTING AND LONG-ACTING INSULIN USE:

🐾 People who take three shots per day sometimes take their NPH at bedtime rather than at dinner to help it last through the night.

🐾 When using insulin glargine (Lantus):

• the dose must be taken alone without any other insulin in the syringe. Then Humalog or NovoLog are taken before each meal.

• the action is very flat and the chance for a bad low blood sugar, particularly during the night, is reduced.

• it works as a basal insulin which prevents the liver from releasing sugar (and ketones) into the blood.

• the dose is determined by the basis of the morning blood sugar no matter when the Lantus shot is taken (a.m., lunch, dinner or bedtime; all times work - though one consistent time must be chosen). If the blood sugar is consistently above the desired range (Chapter 7) at breakfast, the dose is increased. If below the lower level, the dose is decreased.

☙ The intermediate-acting insulins (NPH, Ultralente, Lente) act as basal insulins plus their action peaks help to lower the blood sugar after eating food.

☙ **EXAMPLE OF INSULIN USE FOR A DAY:**

Breakfast: Humalog or NovoLog (with or without NPH).

Lunch: If NPH is not taken at breakfast, a shot of Humalog or NovoLog will be needed.

Dinner: Humalog or NovoLog.

Morning, dinner or bedtime: Lantus is given alone in the syringe at the time instructed by the health care provider. It can be taken (alone) in the morning, at dinner or at bedtime. As noted above, the dose of Lantus is based on the pattern of morning blood sugar levels.

Figure 2: Use of Lantus Insulin
Two of the most common methods of using Lantus insulin:

In the first example, Lantus is used as the basal insulin and Humalog (H) or NovoLog is taken prior to meals.

In this second example, NPH and Humalog (H) or NovoLog are taken in one syringe in the a.m. Humalog is taken alone at dinner. Lantus (alone in the syringe) is taken either at dinner, at bedtime or in the a.m.

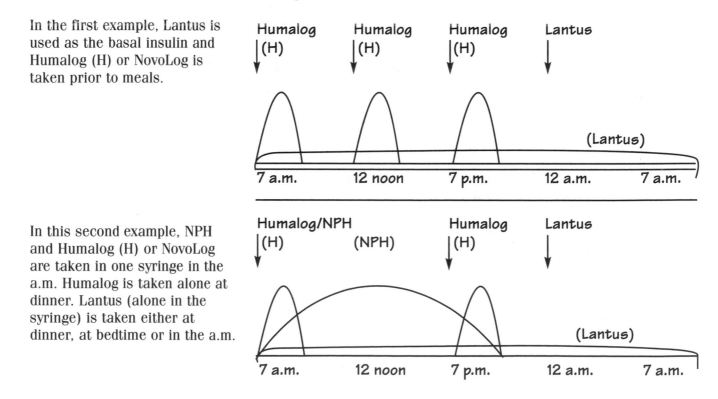

INSULIN ACTIVITIES

Type of Insulin	Begins Working	Main Effect	All Gone
SHORT-ACTING			
Humalog/NovoLog	10-15 minutes	30-90 minutes	4 hours
Regular	30-60 minutes	2-4 hours	6-9 hours
INTERMEDIATE-ACTING			
NPH	2-4 hours	6-8 hours	12-15 hours
Ultralente	4-6 hours	6-12 hours	15-18 hours
LONG-ACTING			
LANTUS (insulin glargine)	1-2 hours	2-24 hours	24 hours
PRE-MIXED INSULINS			
Lente (3 parts Semilente and 7 parts Ultralente)	1-2 hours	6-12 hours	15-24 hours
NPH/Regular (R) mix	30-60 minutes	R = 2-4 hours NPH = 6-8 hours	12-15 hours

Where to inject the insulin.

Chapter 9 DRAWING UP INSULIN AND INSULIN INJECTIONS

The nurse-educator will teach the best way to draw up and give the insulin. Both are described below:

DRAWING UP INSULIN

A. <u>Get everything you will need:</u>

• a bottle of each insulin you will use

• syringe

• alcohol wipe for tops of bottles

• log book with current tests and insulin dose: please record each blood sugar result and insulin dose in log book

B. <u>What to do:</u>

• Know how much of each insulin you need to give (based on "thinking" scales if appropriate – see Chapter 12 in <u>Understanding Diabetes</u>).

• Wipe off the tops of insulin bottles with alcohol swab.

• Inject air into the intermediate-acting (cloudy) insulin bottle with the bottle sitting upright on the table and remove the needle.*

• Inject air in the clear (short-acting) insulin bottle and leave the needle in the bottle.*

• Turn the short-acting bottle with the needle in it upside down and get rid of any air bubbles. (See this chapter for specific steps which can be used to get rid of air bubbles.) Draw up the clear (short-acting) insulin you need and remove the needle from the bottle.

• Mix the cloudy (long-acting) insulin by gently turning the bottle up and down 20 times; this mixes the insulin so that it will have a constant strength.

• Turn the bottle upside down and put the needle into the bottle. Draw up the cloudy insulin into the syringe. ***Make sure not to push any short-acting insulin already in the syringe back into this bottle.***

• If the insulin bottles have been in the refrigerator, you can warm up the insulin once it is mixed in the syringe by holding the syringe in the closed palm of your hand for a minute. It will be less likely to sting if the insulin is at room temperature.

*An option now used by some people is to not put air into the bottles, but to just "vent" the bottles once a week to remove any vacuum. This is done by removing the plunger from the syringe and inserting the needle into the upright insulin vial.

GIVING THE INSULIN

🐾 Choose the area of the body where you are going to give the shot. Use two or more areas and use different sites within the area.

🐾 Make sure the area where you will be giving the shot is clean.

🐾 Relax the chosen area.

🐾 Pull up the skin with the finger and thumb (even with short needles).

🐾 Touch the needle to the skin and gently push it through the skin.

• use a 45° angle for the 5/8 inch needle
(a 45° angle looks like this: ✔__)

• a 90° angle for the 5/16 inch (short) needle: (these hurt less and are not as likely to go into muscle)
(a 90° angle looks like this: ↓)

🐾 Let go of the skin pulled up.

🐾 Push in the insulin slowly and steadily, wait five to 10 seconds to let the insulin spread out.

🐾 Put a finger or dry cotton over the needle as it is pulled out; gently rub a few times to close the hole where the needle was inserted; press your finger or the cotton down on the area where you gave the shot if bruising or bleeding happens.

🐾 Look to see if a drop of insulin comes back through the hole the needle made ("leak-back"); make a note in your log book if this happens.

The nurse will teach the right way to give shots so that a drop of insulin does not leak-back. A drop can contain as much as five units of insulin.

A. Wash hands

B. Warm and mix insulin

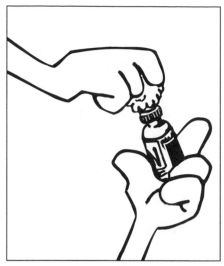

C. Wipe top of insulin bottle with alcohol

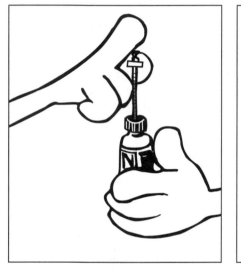

D. Air = insulin dose in units

E. Pull out dose of insulin

F. Make sure injection site is clean

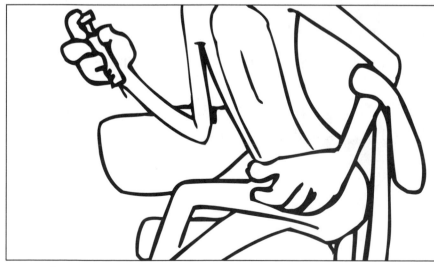

G. Pinch up skin and fat tissue if using 5/8 inch needle.
Go straight in (or pinch) if using the 5/16 inch (short) needle.

H. Inject insulin at 45° (5/8 inch) or 90° (5/16 inch needle)

CHILDREN AND INSULIN SHOTS

🐾 A young child can help with choosing where the shot will be given and by holding still.

🐾 Children usually begin to give some of their own shots around age 10.

🐾 It is important that both mom and dad share in giving shots.

🐾 Some age-related issues (see Chapter 18) are:

Toddlers:

• This age group can sometimes fight when having to get shots. The Inject-Ease® is a device which helps some families.

• Keep the area where the shot will be given as still as possible. Try to get the child's attention on something else (e.g., television, blowing bubbles, looking at a book, etc.). This will help the child to relax.

• The buttocks are often used first, and later the legs and arms and tummy.

• With the child's permission, the Lantus insulin can be given when the child is asleep.

• The parent must remember when giving their child a shot they are giving them health.

School age:

• The child may help in choosing the area on their body to give the shot.

• Change where the shots are given. Use two or more areas and use different sites within the area.

Teens:

• Many teens give their own shots and do not want help.

• It is still important to give the shots in a place (e.g., the kitchen) where parents can actually see the shot given.

• Parents can stay involved by helping to get the supplies out, helping to keep records and writing down the blood sugars and insulin doses each day (in the log book).

Stay in control. You can do it.

Anger, shock, and denial are common feelings
when you first learn you have diabetes.

Chapter 10

FEELINGS AND DIABETES

You and your child will have many feelings when you find out about the diabetes. Having these feelings is very normal. It is important for families to share and talk about these feelings.

The most common feelings are:

- **shock**
- **denial**
- **sadness**
- **anger**
- **fear**
- **guilt**
- **adapting:** as time passes, everyone will not feel so overwhelmed

We ask **EVERY** newly diagnosed family to meet with a counselor to discuss feelings. It is important for all family members to share how they feel. All family members need to work toward feeling positive about how diabetes will fit into their family life.

As time passes, the family will find they are better able to deal with the shots, blood sugar checks, food plan and other day-to-day tasks. More talking within the family and with their health care givers can help reduce the stress.

Fitting the diabetes into as normal a lifestyle as possible becomes the major goal.

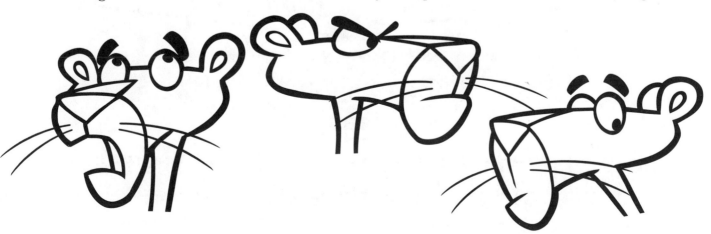

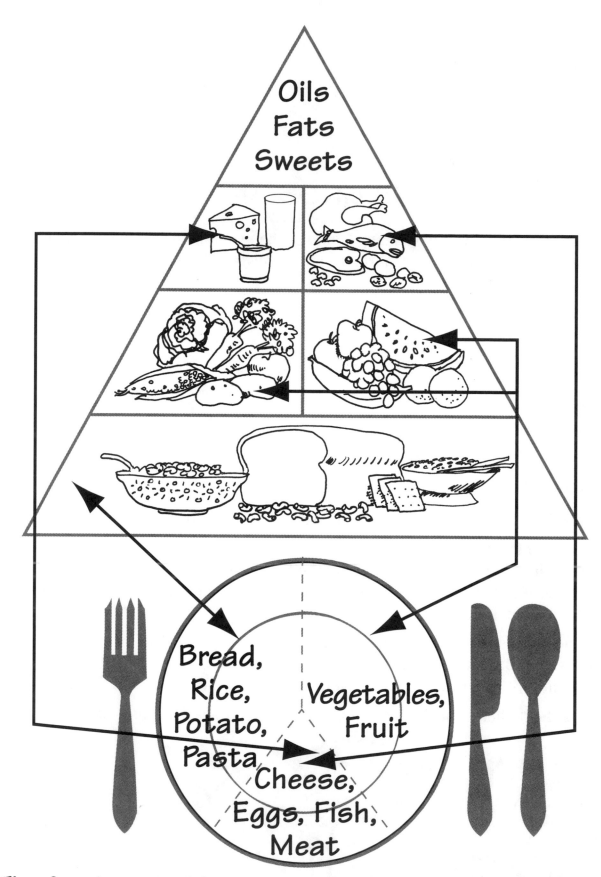

The food pyramid — try to eat more of the foods in the lower three blocks.

Chapter NORMAL NUTRITION

Some knowledge of normal nutrition helps when working with the dietitian on a diabetes food plan.

The foods we eat are divided into:

- **proteins**

- **carbohydrates (includes all sugars)**

- **fats**

- **vitamins and minerals**

- **water**

- **fiber**

All of these are important for our bodies and are discussed in more detail in *Understanding Diabetes*.

Insulin has its main effect on sugars. It is important to only eat high-sugar foods when there is enough insulin acting in the body.

It used to be thought that simple sugars (e.g., candy) were quickly absorbed in the stomach and complex sugars (e.g., starch) were slowly absorbed. This is now known **NOT** to be true. All carbohydrates are used at the same rate so they increase blood sugars in the same way.

Remember, **"a carbohydrate is a carbohydrate is a carbohydrate..."**

It is more important to think about the following:

- **WHEN** carbohydrate is eaten.
  (Do not constantly snack between meals, or else blood sugars will be high.)

- **HOW MUCH** carbohydrate is eaten.
  (A can of sugar pop has 10 teaspoons of sugar and is a "load" for anyone.)

- **WITH WHAT** the carbohydrate is eaten.
  (Other foods slow the sugar absorption.)

- **IF INSULIN IS ACTING** at the same time the sugar is eaten, which allows the carbohydrate to pass into cells for energy (see Chapter 2).

 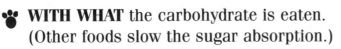

• Working with the dietitian helps families keep up-to-date on new dietary ideas.

• Learning to read nutrition labels on foods at the store can be very helpful. This is discussed in more detail in Chapter 11 of _Understanding Diabetes_.

Having a normal level of blood fats is important for people with diabetes. These levels can be tested at a clinic visit. Suggested levels are given in Chapter 11 of _Understanding Diabetes_.

Eating good foods will help all family members.

Chapter 12 FOOD MANAGEMENT AND DIABETES

A food plan is important for people with either type 1 or type 2 diabetes. Every family must work out a plan with their dietitian that fits their family.

Type 1 diabetes <u>cannot</u> be treated with diet alone.

People with type 2 diabetes:

🐾 can sometimes be treated with diet and exercise alone

🐾 need to eat foods with fewer calories each day and lose weight

• reducing fat calories is especially important (fat has **nine calories** per gram; carbohydrate [carbs] and protein have **four calories** per gram)

• eating no more than once a week at fast food restaurants (burger, fries, pizza) will help

The two types of food plans that our clinic uses the most are:

🐾₁ **constant carbohydrate:** A family often starts with this plan.

• This plan involves eating about the same amount of carbs for each meal and for each snack from day-to-day.

• Insulin doses are changed based on the blood sugar level ("sliding scale"), exercise and other factors such as illness, stress, menses, etc. ("thinking scale").

🐾₂ **carbohydrate ("carb") counting:** Families often move to this plan at a later date.

• This plan involves counting the grams of carbohydrate (carb) in food to be eaten. An amount of short-acting insulin is given which matches the number of grams (gms) of carbohydrate (I/C ratio = insulin to carb ratio).

• The healthcare team and family choose an insulin-to-carb ratio (I/C ratio).

• The dietitian may want a three-day diet record to be done first.

• The ratio which is often used when starting this plan is one unit of insulin for each 15 gms of carbohydrate (I/C ratio of 1 to 15).

• Blood sugars are then done 2 hours after meals to see if the I/C ratio is correct.

If the blood sugar level is high (e.g., over 180 mg/dl or 10 mmol/L), the ratio could be changed to one unit of insulin for 10 gms of carbs (I/C ratio of 1 to 10).

If the blood sugar level is low (e.g., less than 60 mg/dl or 3.3 mmol/L), the ratio could be changed to one unit of insulin for 20 gms of carbs (I/C ratio of 1 to 20).

• Gradually the correct ratios for each meal are found. The I/C ratio may vary between meals.

• A blood sugar is done and an insulin dose "correction factor" (see Chapter 21) is usually added to the I/C ratio dose. This will be the total dose of insulin to be given before the meal or snack.

Several tables of the carb contents of foods and more details about carb counting are found in Chapter 12 of _Understanding Diabetes_.

Some beginning rules of good food management, some of which relate more to a constant carb food plan, are:

• eat a well-balanced diet

• keep the diet similar from day-to-day

• eat meals and snacks at the same time each day

• use snacks to prevent insulin reactions (see suggested snacks in Chapter 12 of _Understanding Diabetes_)

• carefully watch how much carbohydrate is eaten

• avoid over-treating low blood sugars

• eat less cholesterol and saturated fat foods; reduce total fat which is eaten

• keep appropriate growth

• watch weight for height; avoid becoming overweight

• increase the amount of fiber eaten

• eat fewer foods which are high in salt (sodium)

• avoid eating too much protein

A study known as the **DCCT*** found six dietary factors which made sugar control better:

1. following some sort of a meal plan

2. not eating extra snacks

3. not over-treating low blood sugars (hypoglycemia)

4. prompt treatment of high blood sugars when found

5. adjusting insulin levels for meals

6. consistency of bedtime snacks

As shown in the diagram in Chapter 14, food is one of the four major influences on blood sugar control.

*DCCT: Diabetes Control and Complications Trial (see Chapter 14).

Make sure you eat a bedtime snack that has solid protein, fat and carbohydrate.

Getting plenty of exercise is important for everyone.

Chapter 13

EXERCISE AND DIABETES

Regular exercise is important for everyone. It may be more important for people with diabetes. For people with type 2 diabetes, regular exercise and eating less food are two of the most important parts of treating the diabetes (see Chapter 4).

Exercise:

* is one of the "big four," along with insulin or oral medicines, food and stress which affect blood sugar levels (see figure in Chapter 14).

* may raise the blood sugar level (due to adrenaline output). Over-all it helps to keep the blood sugars in a good range. It does this, in part, by making us more sensitive to insulin (see below).

* is a primary part of treating type 2 diabetes.

* should be done daily for at least 30 minutes by people with type 1 or type 2 diabetes.

* can cause **low blood sugars** (Chapter 6) so it is important to plan ahead.

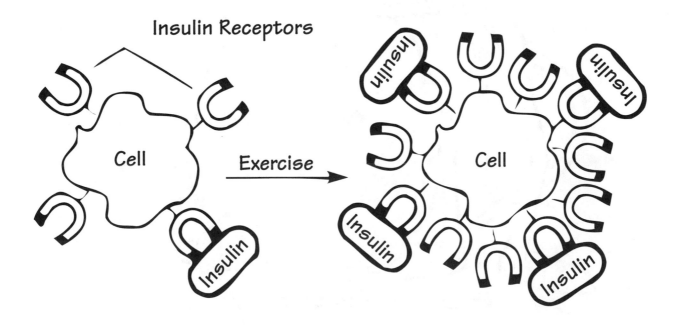

Insulin Receptors

The following may help:

• Extra snacks or less insulin may be needed.

• Preventing low blood sugars during or several hours after ("delayed hypoglycemia") the exercise.
  ~ The PM insulin dose may need to be reduced.
  ~ Adding an extra 15 or 30 grams of carbohydrate at bedtime if afternoon or evening exercise has been strenuous.

• Use of drinks such as Gatorade® during hard exercise.

• Doing extra blood sugar tests can also be very helpful.

• Drinking extra water during exercise prevents dehydration.

🐾 Regular exercise may also be important for people with diabetes in helping to keep normal foot circulation in later years.

Exercise can be fun . . .

. . . and wet!

Learn to balance food, insulin (or oral medicines), stress, and exercise for good sugar control.

Chapter 14 DIABETES AND BLOOD SUGAR CONTROL

People with diabetes whose blood sugars are mostly in the desired range for age are said to be in "good sugar control" (blood sugar is the same thing as blood glucose). Goals for blood sugars are given in this chapter and Chapter 7.

SUGAR CONTROL:

- is measured day-to-day by checking blood sugar levels on a meter
- is also measured by a very important test called the hemoglobin A_{1c} test (HbA_{1c} or A_{1c}).

The HbA_{1c} test:

- can be thought of as the "**forest**" and the blood sugars as the "**trees**"

- tells how often the sugars have been high for every second of the day for the past 90 days

- should be done every three months

- should be in the desired range (see table) for a person to be in "good sugar control"

WHY IS GOOD SUGAR CONTROL IMPORTANT?

Good Sugar Control (lower HbA_{1c} values):

- helps people feel better.
- can lessen the risk for the eye, kidney, and nerve problems from diabetes. This was proven by The **DCCT** (**D**iabetes **C**ontrol and **C**omplications **T**rial).
- helps to lower blood fats (cholesterol and triglyceride levels - Chapter 11).
- helps children grow to their full adult height.

Four factors that influence sugar control (see figure) are:

- **insulin dose or oral medicines**
- **diet**
- **exercise**
- **stress**

These must be in balance for the best possible sugar control.

Table NORMAL RANGES AND GOALS FOR HbA$_{1c}$ AND BLOOD SUGAR VALUES

	HbA$_{1c}$*	Blood Sugar**
Normal values (non-diabetic):	4.3-6.2%	70-120 (3.96-6.6)
Goals for someone with diabetes:		
21 years or older	less than 7%	70-140 (3.9-7.8)
12-21 years	less than 7.8%	70-150 (3.9-8.3)
5-11 years	less than 8%	70-180 (3.9-10)
under five years old	7.5-9%	80-200 (4.5-11)

*Some care providers are now suggesting all children should aim for an HbA$_{1c}$ below 8%, and adults should aim for a level below 7%.

** Blood sugar values are given in mg/dl with the mmol/L in parentheses. These levels should be the goal for both fasting (e.g., AM) and two hours after meals.

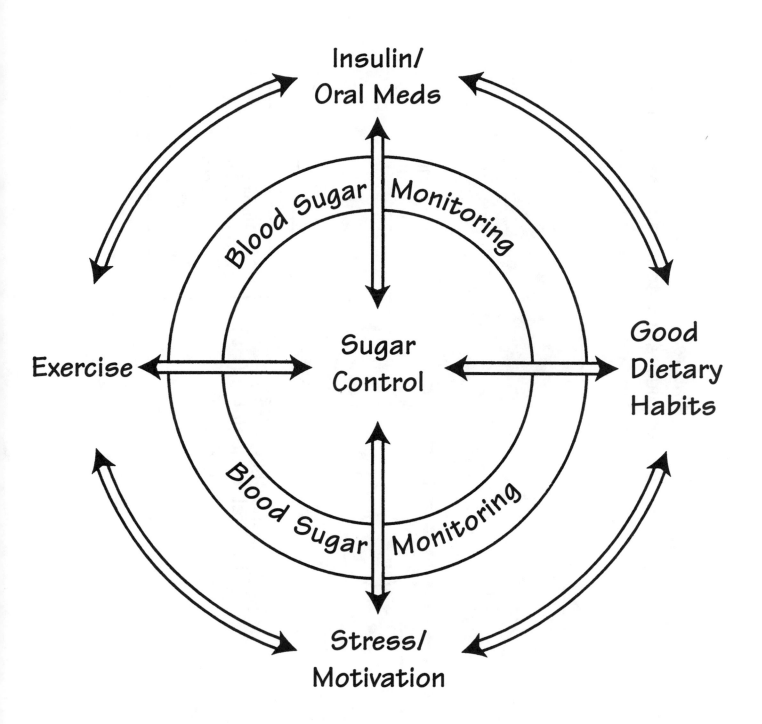

There are four major influences on blood sugar control. All four must be in balance for the best sugar control. Blood sugar control is measured by daily blood sugar levels and by Hemoglobin A_{1c} (HbA_{1c}, A_{1c}) levels done every three months.

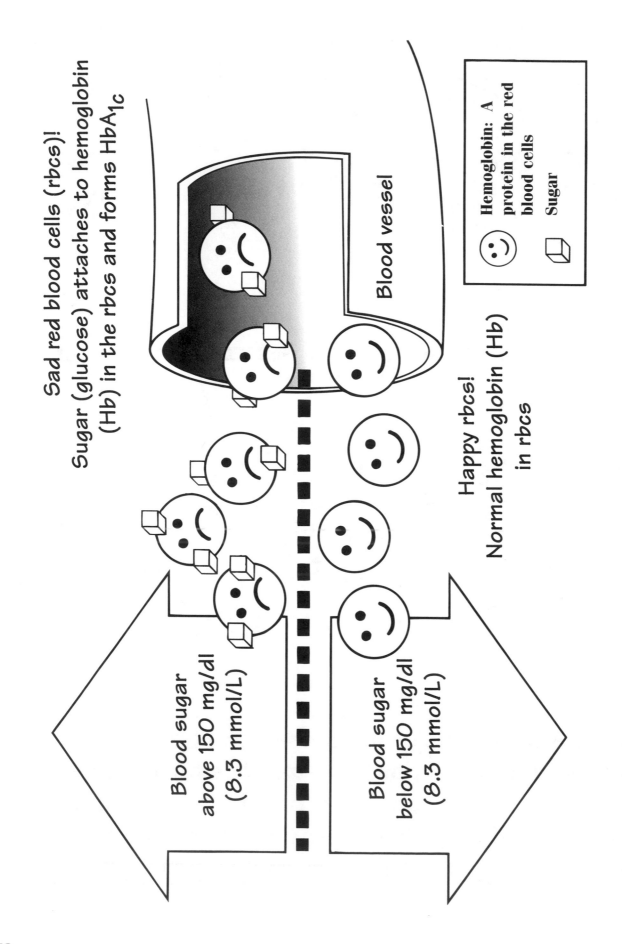

Sad red blood cells (rbcs)!
Sugar (glucose) attaches to hemoglobin (Hb) in the rbcs and forms HbA$_{1c}$

Blood vessel

Happy rbcs!
Normal hemoglobin (Hb) in rbcs

Hemoglobin: A protein in the red blood cells

Sugar

Blood sugar above 150 mg/dl (8.3 mmol/L)

Blood sugar below 150 mg/dl (8.3 mmol/L)

Chapter 15

KETONURIA AND ACIDOSIS (DIABETIC KETOACIDOSIS OR DKA)

This is the second emergency (the other being low blood sugar) of type 1 diabetes.

WHAT LEADS TO DKA?

DKA occurs when *ketones* build up in the body because there isn't enough insulin.

Ketones are:

• made by the body from breaking down fat when sugar cannot be used for energy (not enough insulin in the body)

• an acid that forms when the body uses fat for the energy it needs

HOW DOES IT START?

• The body will first spill ketones in the urine **(ketonuria)** when there isn't enough insulin.

• If the body still doesn't get the insulin it needs, then the ketone (acid) level in the blood builds up (**DKA**: **D**iabetic **K**eto**A**cidosis).

High blood sugar will make you thirsty.

WHAT ARE THE MAIN CAUSES OF KETONURIA OR OF DKA?

1. Forgetting to give one or more insulin shots. Giving "spoiled" insulin (insulin which got too hot [over 90°] or froze).

2. Illness: the amount of insulin needed is usually more so the body will have the extra energy it needs to fight the illness.

3. Not enough insulin (dose too small).

4. An insulin pump which is not working or has been disconnected from the body.

5. Traumatic stress on the body (particularly type 2 diabetes).

DKA can be very dangerous. It usually does not occur unless large urine ketones or blood ketones above 3.0 mmol/L have been present for several hours. It usually occurs in people with known diabetes who forget to check blood or urine ketones as suggested (see below).

WHAT SHOULD BE DONE TO PREVENT DKA?

- check for blood or urine ketones:

- any time the morning blood sugar is above 240 mg/dl (13.3 mmol/L)

- any time the blood sugar is above 300 mg/dl (16.6 mmol/L) at any time of day

- with any illness **(even vomiting one time)**

- Call the diabetes care provider immediately if urine ketones are found to be moderate or large or if the blood ketones are above 1.5 mmol/L.

- When moderate or large urine ketones or blood ketones above 1.0 mmol/L are found, extra short-acting insulin is given every two to three hours to help stop ketones from being made.

- The family should then make repeat calls every two to three hours to the doctor or nurse. Extra doses of short-acting insulin will be needed until the high blood ketones or the moderate or large urine ketones are gone.

- It is also important to drink extra liquids. The extra liquids help to wash out the ketones.

- It is best **NOT** to exercise as the ketone level may increase. When the blood sugar is below 150 mg/dl (8.3 mmol/L), juices and other liquids with sugar can be added.

- It is important to keep the blood sugar level up so that enough insulin can be given to turn off ketone production without having low blood sugar.

- People taking Glyburide (metformin) should stop this medicine until the illness is over.

We have found that DKA can be prevented 95% of the time if the instructions in this chapter are followed.

WHAT ARE THE SIGNS OF DKA?

• Usually the **blood sugar is high**. High blood sugars cause thirst and frequent urination.

• A stomachache, vomiting or a sweet odor to the breath can occur with high ketones.

• Large urine ketones or blood ketones above 3.0 mmol/L have been present for many hours, deep or troubled breathing can occur. This is a sign to go to the emergency room.

High blood sugar will make you go to the bathroom more often.

SUMMARY: PREVENTION OF KETOACIDOSIS (DKA)

WHAT ARE KETONES?

Ketones are the "by-product" made by the body when it uses fat as its energy source.

WHY IS KNOWING ABOUT KETONES IMPORTANT?

If ketones build-up in the body to high levels, they can cause a serious emergency condition called Diabetic KetoAcidosis or DKA.

WHY ARE KETONES SO DANGEROUS?

Ketones are an acid and if their level becomes too high, some parts or systems in the body will not work very well in this 'acid-polluted' environment.

WHEN TO CHECK FOR KETONES:

• with any infection or illness

• if the blood sugar level is high (greater than 300 mg/dl [16.7 mmol/L])

• if the following symptoms are present: vomiting, deep breathing, stomachache, dry mouth or tongue, frequent passage of urine and a 'fruity' odor to the breath

• an insulin shot is missed or the insulin has spoiled (became too hot, too cold or expired)

• with a blockage of an insulin pump catheter or a pump failure

HOW TO CHECK FOR KETONES:

Blood sample: the most important ketone (called beta-hydroxybutyrate [ß-OHB]) can be measured with the Precision Xtra™ meter. The blood ketone test result is given as a number and is the most accurate method to use.

Urine sample: checking a urine sample using a urine dipstick test such as Ketostix™ that measures a different ketone (called acetoacetic acid). Then compare the color of the pad on the stick with the color chart. The test result is read as negative, trace, small, moderate, large or very large.

** One research study found that families were more likely to test for ketones with illness if they used the **blood/meter** (91%) as compared with those using a urine dipstick (56%).*

COMPARISON OF BLOOD AND URINE KETONE READINGS

Blood Ketone (mmol/L)	Urine Ketone Strip color	Level	Action to take
less than 0.6	slight/no color change	negative	normal - no action needed
0.6 to 1.5	light purple	small to moderate**	extra insulin & fluids***
1.6 to 3.0	dark purple	usually large	call MD or RN**
greater than 3.0	very dark purple	very large	**go directly to the E.R.**

It is usually advised to call a health care provider for a blood ketone level greater than 1.5 or with urine ketone readings of moderate or large.

***If the blood glucose level is below 150 mg/dl (8.3 mmol/L), a liquid with glucose should be taken.**

Check your ketones before calling your doctor
when you aren't feeling well.

Chapter 16 SICK-DAY AND SURGERY MANAGEMENT

SICK-DAY MANAGEMENT

Children with diabetes get sick just like other children. The average child gets eight colds a year. These may affect the diabetes.

It is important to:

🐾 Always check **urine and/or blood ketones** and the **blood sugar** with any illness.

• Call your doctor or nurse if the urine ketone result is moderate or large. Also call if the blood ketone level (using the Precision Xtra™ meter) is above 1.5 mmol/L.

• The earlier you treat the ketones with extra Humalog/NovoLog or Regular insulin and fluids, the less chance your child will have to go into the hospital.

🐾 **Always give some insulin.**

• If vomiting is present and ketones are negative, the dose may have to be lowered, but some insulin **must** be given.

• If the person vomits three or more times, a Phenergan suppository may be helpful.

🐾 Glucagon can be mixed and given with an insulin syringe just like insulin.

• It is helpful when the blood sugar is low and vomiting continues.

• The dose is one unit for every year of age up to 18 units.

• It should <u>not</u> be given if ketones are moderate or large.

• Call your doctor or nurse before giving the glucagon injection if you have questions.

🐾 Many medications have a warning label that a person with diabetes should not use the medicine. This is because they may raise the blood sugar a few points.

• Our view is that if the medicine is needed, go ahead and take it. We can always give a bit more insulin if needed.

• Steroids (e.g., prednisone) are the most difficult (often used for asthma) and, if prescribed, the diabetes care provider should be notified.

😾 Youth with type 2 diabetes must also remember to check the urine and/or blood ketone level.

• If the person is receiving Glyburide (metformin), the pills should be stopped during the illness. (A condition called lactic acidosis can develop.)

• It is usually best to return to insulin shots during the illness.

• Call your doctor or nurse if you have questions.

SURGERY MANAGEMENT

If surgery is planned:

😾 Call your diabetes care provider **AFTER** you find out the time of the surgery and if eating food in usual amounts will be allowed.

😾 Take your own diabetes supplies with you to the surgery:

• glucose meter and strips

• insulin and syringes

• glucose tablets or gel

• blood ketone strips or urine Ketostix

• glucagon emergency kit

• if on a pump, equipment to change insertions if needed

😾 Take your phone card with your diabetes care provider's numbers.

😾 If you/your child received a basal insulin (e.g.: by insulin pump or by Lantus injection), the basal insulin can be continued during the period of surgery. Then restart bolus pump therapy or other insulins when the person is able to eat.

MANAGEMENT OF VOMITING (*WITHOUT* KETONES)

Table 1

Avoid solid foods until the vomiting has stopped.

If vomiting is frequent, some doctors recommend giving a Phenergan suppository to reduce vomiting and waiting to give fluids for an hour until the suppository is working.

If you do not have suppositories, ask for a prescription for them at the time of your clinic visit.

Gradually start liquids (juice, Pedialyte®, water, etc.) in small amounts. Juices (especially orange) replace the salts that are lost with vomiting or diarrhea. Pedialyte popsicles are also available.

🐾 Start with a tablespoon of liquid every 10-20 minutes.

🐾 If the blood sugar is below 100 mg/dl (5.5 mmol/L):

   • Sugar pop can be given.

   • For some children, sucking on a piece of hard candy often works well.

   • If the blood sugar is below 70 mg/dl (3.9 mmol/L), give glucagon just as you would give insulin. The dose is 1 unit per year of age up to 18 units. Repeat doses can be given every 20 minutes as needed.

🐾 If the blood sugar is above 150 mg/dl (8.3 mmol/L):

   • Do not give pop with sugar in it.

🐾 If there is no further vomiting, gradually increase the amount of fluid.

🐾 If vomiting restarts, it may again be necessary to rest the stomach for another hour and then restart the small amounts of fluids. A repeat suppository can be given after three or four hours.

After a few hours without vomiting, gradually return to a normal diet. Soups are often good to start with and they provide needed nutrients.

SICK-DAY FOODS

Liquids

- Fruit juice: apple, cranberry, grape, grapefruit, orange, pineapple, etc.

- Sugar containing beverages: regular 7Up®, gingerale, orange juice, cola, PEPSI®, etc.*

- Fruit flavored drinks: regular Kool-Aid, lemonade, Hi-C®, etc.

- Sports drinks: Gatorade, POWERāDE®, etc., any flavor

- Tea with honey or sugar

- Pedialyte or Infalyte® (especially for younger children)

- JELL-O®: regular (for infants, liquid JELL-O warmed in a bottle) or diet*

- Popsicles, regular or diet*

- Broth type soup: bouillon, chicken noodle soup, Cup-a-Soup®

Solids (when ready)

- Saltine crackers

- Banana (or other fruit)

- Applesauce

- Bread or toast

- Graham crackers

- Soup

Sugar free may be needed depending on blood sugars (e.g., greater than 150 mg/dl [8.3 mmol/L]).

Table **3**

SICK-DAY MANAGEMENT: WHEN TO CALL FOR EMERGENCY CARE

• If you have vomited more than three times and can keep nothing in your stomach, and urine ketones are not moderate or large or blood ketones above 1.5 mmol/L, call your primary care physician.

• *If help is needed with an insulin dose, call your diabetes care provider.*

• If moderate or large ketones are present or blood ketones are above 1.5 mmol/L, call your diabetes care provider.

• If you have difficulty breathing or have "deep breathing," you need to go to an emergency room. This usually indicates severe acidosis (ketoacidosis).

• If there is any unusual behavior such as confusion, slurred speech, double vision, inability to move or talk, or jerking, someone should give sugar or instant glucose. (Glucagon [Chapter 6] is given if the person is unconscious or if a convulsion [seizure] occurs.) The diabetes care provider should be contacted if a severe reaction occurs. In case of a convulsion or loss of consciousness, it may be necessary to call the paramedics or to go to an emergency room. Have an emergency number posted by the phone.

When you/your child are ill ...

Start here

Always check blood sugar (B.S.) and ketones (urine or blood)

Blood sugar is within target range and ketones are negative

- Continue to check blood sugars and ketones every 3-4 hrs
- Call for appt. with primary MD if fever or infection is present

---

B.S. greater than 250 and urine ketones are **mod/large** *or* blood ketones **greater than 1.0**

Repeat if needed *(ketones still elevated)*

- Give 10-20% of **total** daily insulin dose using Humalog *or* NovoLog*
- Give non-sugar fluids as tolerated
- Recheck B.S. and ketones every 2 hrs

B.S. 150-250 and urine ketones are **mod/large** *or* blood ketones **greater than 1.0**

Repeat if needed *(ketones still elevated)*

- Give 10-20% of **total** daily insulin dose using Humalog *or* NovoLog*
- Give fluids (with some sugar) as tolerated
- Recheck B.S. and ketones every 2 hrs

B.S. less than 150 and urine ketones are **mod/large** *or* blood ketones **greater than 1.0**

- Give fluids with sugar
- Recheck B.S. and ketones every 1-2 hrs
- May need extra insulin **when B.S. is greater than 150**

-If ketones are still elevated

For Vomiting

- Wait 30-45 min., then give clear fluid sips every 15 min. as tolerated (with sugar if B.S. less than 150)
- If increased ketones, will need insulin if B.S. greater than 150*

---

*Extra rapid-acting insulin given (every 2-3 hrs) until ketones are negative and B.S. in target range.

Some families double their correction insulin dose rather than using 10-20% of the total daily insulin dose.

IF URINE KETONES ARE LARGE OR BLOOD KETONES ARE GREATER THAN 1.5, CALL YOUR DIABETES CARE PROVIDER.

Your insulin dose may change when you are sick,
but you *always* need some insulin.

Family support is very important to
the child with diabetes.

Chapter 17 FAMILY CONCERNS

Diabetes is a family disease. This means that all family members must help. The children who do best with their diabetes have the help and support of their parents and family members.

🐾 It is important for children with diabetes to be treated just like other children. A good rule to follow is:

THINK OF THE CHILD FIRST AND THEN THE DIABETES.

🐾 It is important that all family members share their feelings (see Chapter 10).

🐾 Siblings often feel left out when the child with diabetes needs more attention.

🐾 This should be discussed with the other children and time should be set aside for them as well.

🐾 Perhaps the most supportive and loving act that parents, brothers and sisters can make for the person with diabetes is to remove high-sugar foods (candy, sugar pop, donuts, cookies, etc.) from the home. These foods have little nutritional value. If they are around, they may be eaten without taking extra insulin, which will raise the blood sugar.

SPECIFIC AREAS OF CONCERN

🐾① The stress of the diagnosis of diabetes is real for all family members.

One of the four big influences on blood sugar levels is stress (see Chapter 14). The social worker or psychologist is available to help in dealing with stress.

🐾② Extra excitement and activity may cause a low blood sugar in children with diabetes. Some of these activities can include:

- family picnics

- sleepovers

- trips to the beach or hiking

- school field days or trips

- a trip to a Disney® or other theme parks

- special days such as Christmas or Hanukkah

Thinking ahead and reducing the insulin dose and giving extra snacks may result in a better day for everyone. Wearing an ID bracelet is particularly important on trips.

3. Needle fears occur in about one-fourth of all people. The psychosocial team may be helpful, particularly in suggesting distractions (TV, toys, books) or relaxation techniques. The Inject-Ease device (B-D) is sometimes helpful.

4. Missed shots (or insulin boluses for the pumper) result in an elevated HbA$_{1c}$ level and an increased risk for diabetic complications. Help from other family members, teachers or friends may be needed.

Social workers and psychologists are there to help you.

Think of the child first and THEN the diabetes.

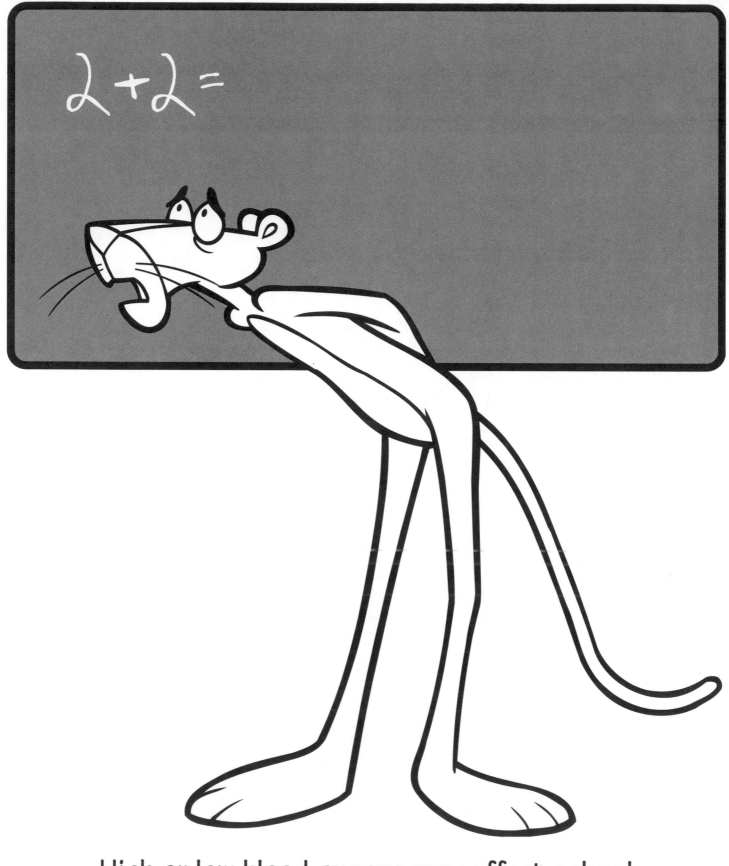

High or low blood sugars may affect school performance.

Chapter 18

RESPONSIBILITIES OF CHILDREN AT DIFFERENT AGES

Children of different ages are able to handle different tasks and responsibilities. These may vary from day-to-day and week-to-week. This is true for diabetes-related tasks and non-diabetes tasks. It can be helpful for family members to have an idea of what to expect at different ages.

(See the tables of age-responsibilities in <u>Understanding Diabetes</u>.)

Below age 8

- Parents do all tasks.

- Children gradually learn to cooperate.

- Shots are often given after meals or snacks depending upon what was eaten.

Ages 8-12

- Children begin to give some of their own shots. A common mistake is to push for too much responsibility before the child is ready.

- Having a friend spend the night or staying at a friend's house often begins during this period. As the children are often very active and use more energy from staying up later than usual, it is best to reduce the insulin dose.

Ages 10-14

- At this age, fine motor control and the sense of accuracy needed to draw up the insulin develops.

- It is important to continue to check doses of insulin drawn by the child and the blood sugar testing meters to review their readings.

- The idea of maintaining good sugar control to prevent later diabetes complications can initially be understood around age 13.

Ages 13-18

One of the most difficult chores for many teens is writing the blood sugar values in a log book. It is important to do this or trends in blood sugar values will be missed. Often the parents agree to do this (with the teen's OK). It is also a way for the parents to stay involved with the diabetes care and to step back in if blood sugars are not being done.

What is the age when self-care should happen?

• Children should be encouraged to assume self-care as they are able.

• There isn't a "magic" age when children should take over everything.

• If too much is expected too soon, feelings of failure and low self-esteem with poor diabetes self-care may result.

It is now believed that a supportive adult can be valuable for any person with diabetes, no matter their age.

An alarm watch may help to remind a child of the need for a snack, or for pumpers to give a bolus of insulin.

Children between the ages of 8-14 can help to
manage their diabetes.

Teenagers have their own special challenges.

Chapter 19

SPECIAL CHALLENGES OF THE TEEN YEARS

The teen years are a time when young people go between wanting to be an independent adult and wanting to stay a dependent child. It is not surprising that they go back and forth when it comes to taking over the diabetes responsibilities. Many research studies now show that when parents stay involved in diabetes management, the diabetes will be in better control.

THE CHALLENGES

- The teen-aged years are often the most difficult for having good sugar control (a good HbA_{1c} level). And yet, they are important years in relation to diabetes complications.

- The teens in the intensive-treatment arm of the DCCT (Chapter 14) often had weekly clinic visits, but still had a mean HbA_{1c} of 8.1% (compared with 7.1% for the adults).

- Growth and sexual hormones are at high levels and interfere with insulin activity.

- Insulin pumps, more frequent insulin shots, and the new basal insulin, insulin glargine (Lantus) can help some teens. However, if meal shots (or boluses for pumpers) are missed, the HbA_{1c} will be high.

- Driving a car safely is very important beginning in the teen years. It is important to check a blood sugar before driving. Driving with a low blood sugar can result in problems that can be just as severe as if driving while drunk.

- Diabetes is often not a priority to the teenager. Teenagers have special issues including:

  - **struggle for independence**

  - **growth and body changes**

  - **self-identity**

  - **peer relationships**

  - **sexuality**

  - **consistency:** is considered a key word in diabetes management. This refers to eating, exercise, stress or times of insulin shots. It is often hard for teens to be consistent.

It is not surprising that diabetes is often referred to as a "disease of compromise."

Parents must:

• **find ways to stay involved in diabetes management.** They can be helpful in keeping the log book and in talking about insulin dosage.

• **be available to help, but should try not to be overbearing or constantly nagging.** A supportive adult can be helpful for a person with diabetes no matter their age.

Teenagers with diabetes can lead normal lives.

Normal teen activities can provide much needed
exercise.

Clinic visits should be every three months for people with diabetes.

Chapter 20

OUTPATIENT MANAGEMENT, EDUCATION, SUPPORT GROUPS AND STANDARDS OF CARE

WHAT SHOULD HAPPEN AFTER A DIAGNOSIS OF DIABETES?

- Regular follow-up visits should be every three months for people with diabetes. Diabetes education should continue for the patient and family at these visits.

- The insulin dose may be changed during these visits. It is usually increased one-half unit per pound of weight gained (just to have the same dose for weight).

- Growth and other signs of sugar control such as liver size and finger curvatures are checked. If blood sugars are high, the sugar collects on the joint proteins and finger curvatures may result.

- On the physical exam, items such as thyroid size and eye changes are checked.

- The HbA$_{1c}$ blood test (see Chapter 14) should be done every three months.

- After having diabetes for three years as a teen or adult, eye exams by an eye doctor and special kidney tests are very important to have each year (see Chapter 22).

- For people with type 2 diabetes, the eye and kidney testes should be done at the time of diagnosis, and then yearly.

WHAT ELSE IS IMPORTANT?

- Communication (fax, e-mail) of blood sugar values to the health care provider is often helpful.

- The families should let their diabetes provider or diabetes team know about any of the following:

  • any severe low blood sugar (hypoglycemic) reactions

  • frequent mild reactions

  • moderate or large urine ketones or blood ketones above 1.5 mmol/L

  • any planned surgery

  • if at least half of the blood sugar values are not in the desired range for age (see Chapter 7)

Support groups and special educational programs (Research Updates, Grandparents Workshop, College-Bound Workshop, etc.) are available in many areas.

Special events (ski trips, bike trips, camping, a Halloween party, etc.) help children and families to learn more about diabetes. They also provide a chance to talk to others who have a family member with diabetes.

Faxing or e-mailing blood sugars to the clinic between visits is very important.

Mark your calendar to remind you of follow-up
visits every three months.

You need to think about your insulin dose.

Chapter 21

ADJUSTING THE INSULIN DOSE, CORRECTION FACTORS, "THINKING" SCALES AND INSULIN "COCKTAILS"

Six to twelve months after the diagnosis of diabetes, many families feel OK with changing the insulin doses.

HOW AND WHEN SHOULD AN INSULIN DOSE BE CHANGED?

Below are four methods:

1. Looking at blood sugar patterns:

🐾 It is necessary to know which insulin is acting at the time of the highs or lows in order to make the correct changes (see figures in Chapter 8).

🐾 If more than half of the blood sugar values at any time of the day are above the desired range for the age of the person (see table in Chapter 7):

• The insulin dose acting at the time of the high sugar value should be increased.

• If values are still high after three days, the dose can be increased again.

🐾 If there are more than two lows (below 60 mg/dl [3.2 mmol/L]) at one time of day:

• The insulin dose acting at that time should be decreased.

• If more lows occur, the dose can be decreased again the next day.

🐾 With small children, the change in dose may be by half a unit.

🐾 With older children, the change in dose may be by one unit.

🐾 Blood sugars will be lowest the first day after an increase in insulin and highest the first day after a decrease in insulin.

2. Using a "correction factor":

🐾 Some people use a combination of a **"correction factor"** and carbohydrate (carb) counting (see Chapter 12) to determine the dose of short-acting insulin before meals and snacks.

🐾 The correction factor can be used to "correct" a high blood sugar down to a target blood sugar level (e.g., 150 mg/dl or 8.3 mmol/L).

- The most common correction factor is to give one unit of insulin for every 50 mg/dl (2.7 mmol/L) of glucose above 150 mg/dl (8.3 mmol/L) [e.g., if the blood sugar is 250, the correction factor would be 2 units]. However, every person is different and the correction factor should be adjusted to fit the individual.

- At bedtime, during the night, or before exercise, the correction factor is usually reduced by half.

- It is generally wise to wait two hours between correction insulin dosages.

3. Using "thinking" scales:

- The insulin dose is figured by considering:

  - the blood sugar level

  - any exercise that has been or is to be done

  - food to be eaten

  - illness

  - stress

  - menses

  - other factors

4. Using insulin "cocktails":

- Insulin "cocktail" refers to the mixtures of three or more insulins in the same syringe. An example of three insulins which might be given together are:

- Humalog or NovoLog and Regular and an intermediate-action insulin (e.g., NPH).

  - The Humalog or NovoLog will help to lower a high morning sugar and cover food eaten for breakfast.

  - The Regular helps to cover the morning snack and the lunch period.

  - The NPH covers the afternoon.

- Two intermediate-action insulins (e.g., NPH and Ultralente) can also be mixed in the same syringe with a short-acting insulin.

EXAMPLE OF INSULIN ADJUSTMENTS

Blood Sugar mg/dl	mmol/L	Correction Factor* Units of Insulin	Carb Choices** (15 gm carb)	Total Units of Insulin
less than 150	8.3	0	1	1
200	11.1	1	2	3
250	13.9	2	3	5
300	16.7	3	4	7
350	19.4	4	5	9

* Assuming a correction factor of 1 unit of short-acting insulin per 50 mg (2.8 mmol/L) above 150 mg/dl (8.3 mmol/L).

** One Carb choice = 15 gm carbohydrate. In this example, 1 unit of insulin is given for each 15 gm carb choice.

The insulin dose and the amount of food eaten may need to change with sports activities.

Have your eyes checked regularly.

Chapter 22   LONG-TERM COMPLICATIONS OF DIABETES

WHAT CAN MAKE THE RISK OF THESE COMPLICATIONS LESS?

🐾 Good sugar control will reduce the risk for eye, kidney, and nerve complications of diabetes by more than 50 percent as shown by the DCCT (Chapter 14).

🐾 Not smoking (or chewing) tobacco also helps.

🐾 Another factor is the blood pressure. Researchers at our Center showed that even mild increases in blood pressure are bad for the eyes and kidneys.

HOW ARE COMPLICATIONS FOUND?

Small blood vessel problems:

• Eye exams (and sometimes photographs) by the eye doctor tell if someone is developing eye damage.

• The *microalbumin* test tells if someone is getting early kidney damage at a time when it may still be reversible. The instructions for doing the microalbumin test to detect early kidney damage are at the end of Chapter 22 in *Understanding Diabetes*. We prefer overnight urine collections as a false positive result is less likely.

• Screening tests for the eyes and kidneys should be done once yearly for people who have had type 1 diabetes for three or more years and have reached puberty (age 10 to 12 years).

• People who have type 2 diabetes should have the eye and kidney tests done soon after diagnosis and then every year.

• Families may need to help remind the health care team that it is time to do the microalbumin test or to see an eye doctor.

• Treatment of early eye or kidney damage is done by improving sugar control.

• Treatment of early kidney damage is also done by lowering blood pressure. A blood pressure medicine called an ACE-inhibitor is often helpful.

• If many eye changes are present, laser treatment to the back of the eye (retina) may help to prevent more severe problems.

Large blood vessel problems in adults:

• Heart attacks and other blood vessel diseases are a greater risk for adults with diabetes.

• Cholesterol levels and a lipid panel should be checked yearly.

• A baby aspirin and a fish oil capsule (omega-3 fatty acid) taken once or twice daily may help in prevention.

TWO OTHER DISEASES WHICH CAN OCCUR IN PEOPLE WITH DIABETES ARE:

Thyroid problems: thyroid problems (like diabetes) are due to autoimmunity (see Chapter 3). Antibodies are made against the thyroid gland.

Celiac disease: this is an allergy to the wheat protein, gluten. It occurs in 1 of every 20 people with diabetes. There may be stomach complaints (pain, gas, diarrhea) or poor growth. Half of the people with celiac disease have no symptoms. The treatment is to remove all wheat, rye and barley products from the diet.

Finger curvatures can be a sign of high blood sugar levels over many years.

DO NOT SMOKE!

SCHOOL DIABETES MANAGEMENT CHECKLIST FOR PARENTS:

_____ Discuss specific care of your child with the teachers, school nurse and other staff who will be involved.

_____ Complete the individualized school health care plan with the help of school staff and your diabetes care staff (see two examples in this chapter).

_____ Make sure your child understands who will help him/her with testing, shots and treatment of high or low blood sugars at school and where supplies will be kept. Supplies should be kept in a place where they are always available if needed.

_____ Keep current phone numbers where you can be reached. Collect equipment for school: meter, strips and finger-poker, lancets, insulin, insulin syringes, biohazard container, log book or a copy of testing record form (make arrangements to have blood sugars sent home routinely), extra insulin pump supplies, ketone testing strips, photo for substitute teacher's folder.

_____ Food and drinks; parents need to check periodically to make sure supplies are not used up:

- juice cans or boxes (approximately 15 grams of carb each)
- glucose tablets
- instant glucose or cake-decorating gel
- crackers(± peanut butter and/or cheese)
- quarters to buy sugar pop if needed
- Fruit Roll-Ups®
- dried fruit
- raisins or other snacks

_____ box with the child's name to store these food and drink items

The school and diabetes.

Chapter 23

THE SCHOOL AND DIABETES

Parents want to know that their child is in safe hands while at school. It is the parents' responsibility (not the child's) to inform and educate the school. Parents also want to make sure their child is not treated differently as a result of having diabetes.

WHAT SHOULD BE DONE?

🐾 Many schools now require school health plans. An individualized school health plan (which you are welcome to copy) is included in this chapter. The parents and diabetes nurse should fill this out. The parents can then go over the plan with the school nurse or aide.

🐾 The parents must also provide supplies for the school. Some children keep a separate meter and strips at the school. Others bring their home meter and supplies in their backpack.

🐾 Other forms that you may want to copy from the larger book are:
1) School Intake Interview
2) Interventions for Emergency Situations
3) Emergency Response Plan
4) Individualize the Health Care Plan Check List for the School Nurse
5) Insulin Pumps in the School Setting
6) A general letter for the principal or school nurse

WHAT CAN HAPPEN AT SCHOOL?

• Low blood sugars are the most likely emergency to occur at school. It may be helpful for the family to copy and review the table on mild, moderate and severe reactions with the school (see Chapter 6). *Supplies for treating lows will also need to be provided by the family.*

• High blood sugars and/or ketones may also occur at school, particularly with stress, illness, overeating or lack of exercise. If the blood sugar is above 300 mg/dl (16.65 mmol/L) the urine or blood ketones need to be checked. When the blood sugar is high it is generally necessary to go to the bathroom more frequently. *If moderate or large urine ketones or blood ketones above 0.6 mmol/L occur, the parents need to be called.*

INDIVIDUALIZED SCHOOL HEALTH CARE PLAN: DIABETES
Date: _____

Student _____ Date of birth _____
School _____ Grade _____ Teacher _____
Parent(s)/Guardian(s) _____
Phone (H) _____ (W) _____ (Other) _____
Additional emergency contact information _____
Diabetes Care Provider _____ Phone _____ Fax _____
Diabetes Nurse Educator _____ Phone _____ Fax _____
Hospital of choice _____
ROUTINE MANAGEMENT Target Blood Sugar Range _____ to _____

Required blood sugar testing at school:
❑ Trained personnel must perform blood sugar test
❑ Trained personnel must supervise blood sugar test
❑ Student can perform testing independently

Times to do blood sugar:
❑ Before lunch
❑ After lunch
❑ Before P.E.
❑ After P.E.
❑ As needed for signs/symptoms of low or high blood sugar

❑ Call parent if values are below _____ or above _____

Medications to be given during school hours:
❑ Oral diabetes medication(s)/dose _____ Time to be administered:_____.
❑ Sliding scale: To be administered immediately:
Insulin (subcutaneous injection) using Humalog / NovoLog / Regular (circle type) <u>Before lunch</u> <u>After lunch</u>
____ Unit(s) if lunch blood sugar is between ____ and ____   ❑   ❑
____ Unit(s) if lunch blood sugar is between ____ and ____   ❑   ❑
____ Unit(s) if lunch blood sugar is between ____ and ____   ❑   ❑
____ Unit(s) if lunch blood sugar is between ____ and ____   ❑   ❑
❑ Insulin/Carb Ratio ____ Unit for every ____ grams of carbohydrate eaten,
   plus ____ unit(s) for every ____ mg/dl points above ____ mg/dl
❑ Student can draw up and inject own insulin   ❑ Student cannot draw up own insulin but can give own injection
❑ Trained adult will draw up and administer injection   ❑ Student can draw up but needs adult to inject insulin
❑ Student is on pump   ❑ Student needs assistance checking insulin dosage
❑ Glucagon (subcutaneous injection) dosage (see Chapter 6); dosage = ____ cc

Diet:
Lunch time _____ Scheduled P.E. time _____ Recess time _____
Snack time(s) ____ a.m. ____ p.m.   Location that snacks are kept _____ Location eaten _____

❑ Child needs assistance with prescribed meal plan (see attached) . Parents/Guardian and student are
responsible for maintaining necessary supplies, snacks, testing kit, medications and equipment.

Field trip information:
1. Notify parent and school nurse in advance so proper training can be accomplished.
2. Adult staff must be trained and responsible for student's needs on field trip.
3. Extra snacks, glucose monitoring kit, copy of health plan, glucose gel or other emergency supplies must
   accompany student on field trip.
4. Adults accompanying student on a field trip will be notified on a need to know basis.

People trained for blood testing and response:
Name _____ Date _____
Name _____ Date _____

Permission signatures:
As parent/guardian of the above named student, I give permission for use of this health plan in my student's
school and for the school nurse to contact the above providers regarding the above condition. Orders are
valid through the end of the current school year.

Parent Signature _____ Date _____
Nurse Signature _____ Date _____
Physician Signature _____ Date _____

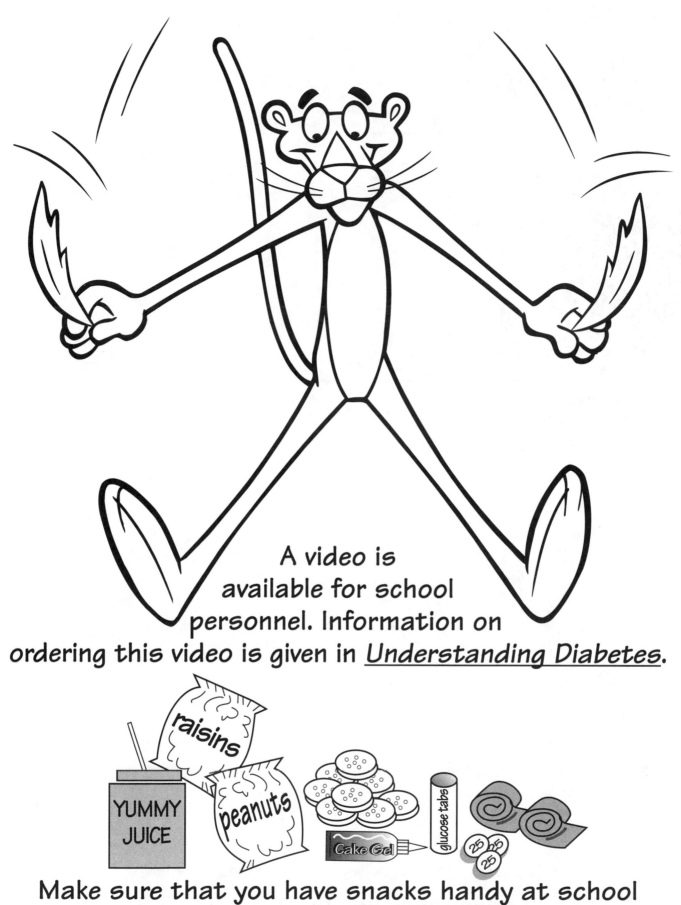

A video is
available for school
personnel. Information on
ordering this video is given in _Understanding Diabetes._

Make sure that you have snacks handy at school
in case you need them.

Keep the emergency list in an easy-to-find place

Chapter 24 BABY-SITTERS, GRANDPARENTS AND OTHER CAREGIVERS

It is important for parents to feel safe when their child is with caregivers other than the parents. It is also important for these caregivers to feel confident that they can do a good job.

WHAT DO THEY NEED TO KNOW?

☙ How much training is needed will depend upon the amount of time the child will be with the caregiver and the age of the child.

All caregivers need:

• some information about signs of low blood sugar and how to treat it. A low blood sugar can occur at any time.

• some basic instruction on foods and diabetes is also important. A two-page handout is in this chapter, which can be cut out or copied for the caregiver.

• emergency phone numbers in case the parents cannot be reached helps everyone feel better.

• to know how to give shots, when to check for urine or blood ketones, and other more detailed information if the parents are to be away for a longer time period.

• an extra supply of insulin, etc. is important (in case a bottle is dropped and broken).

☙ Attending a "Grandparent Workshop" or other workshop can help to teach the grandparents, baby-sitters or other caregivers about diabetes.

• It is important for the child and the grandparents to continue to have a close relationship.

• It can also help to remove any fears about giving shots or treating low blood sugars.

☙ Caregivers may wish to join the parents at initial education classes or at the time of clinic visits. They are always welcome.

INFORMATION FOR THE SITTER OR GRANDPARENT

Our child, _____, has diabetes.

Children with diabetes are generally normal and healthy. In a child who has diabetes, sugar cannot be used by the body because the pancreas no longer makes the hormone insulin. Because of this, daily insulin injections are needed. Diabetes is not contagious. Caring for a child with diabetes is not very difficult, but it does require a small amount of extra knowledge.

Low Blood Sugar

The only emergency that could come on quickly is **LOW BLOOD SUGAR** (otherwise known as "hypoglycemia" or an "insulin reaction"). This can occur if the child gets more exercise than usual or does not eat as much as usual. *The warning signs of low blood sugar vary but include any of the following:* (They are discussed in greater detail in Chapter 6.)

1. Hunger

2. Paleness, sweating, shaking

3. Eyes appear glassy, dilated or "big" pupils

4. Pale or flushed face

5. Personality changes such as crying or stubbornness

6. Headaches

7. Inattention, drowsiness, sleepiness at an unusual time

8. Weakness, irritability, confusion

9. Speech and coordination changes

10. If not treated, loss of consciousness and/or seizure

The signs our child usually has are: _____

_____

_____

BLOOD SUGAR: It is ideal to check the blood sugar if this is possible. It takes 10 minutes for the blood sugar to increase after taking liquids with sugar. Thus, the blood sugar can even be done after taking sugar. If it is not convenient to check the blood sugar, go ahead with treatment anyway.

TREATMENT: Give SUGAR (preferably in a liquid form) to help the blood sugar rise.

You may give any of the following:

1. Soft drink that contains sugar (1/2 cup) - **NOT a diet pop**

2. Three or four glucose tablets, sugar packets or cubes or a teaspoon of honey

3. Fruit juice (1/2 cup)

4. LIFE-SAVERS® candy (FIVE or SIX) if over three years of age

5. One-half tube of Insta-Glucose or cake decorating gel (see below)

We usually treat reactions with: _____

If the child is having an insulin reaction and he/she refuses to eat or has difficulty eating, give Insta-Glucose, cake-decorating gel (1/2 tube) or other sugar (honey or syrup). Put the Insta-Glucose, a little bit at a time, between the cheeks (lips) and the gums and tell the child to swallow. If he/she can't swallow, lay the child down and turn the head to the side so the sugar or glucose doesn't cause choking. You can help the sugar solution absorb by massaging the child's cheek.

If a low blood sugar (insulin reaction) or other problems occur, please call (in order):

1. Parent: _____ at: _____

2. Physician: _____ at: _____

3. Other person: _____ at: _____

🐾 Meals and Snacks

The child must have meals and snacks on time. The schedule is as follows:

	Time	**Food to Give**
Breakfast	_____	_____
Snack	_____	_____
Lunch	_____	_____
Snack	_____	_____
Supper	_____	_____
Snack	_____	_____

Sometimes young children will not eat meals and snacks at exactly the time suggested. If this happens, DON'T PANIC! Set the food within the child's reach (in front of the TV set often works) and leave him/her alone. If the food hasn't been eaten in 10 minutes, give a friendly reminder. Allow about 30 minutes for meals.

🐾 Blood Sugars

It may be necessary to check the blood sugar (Chapter 7) or ketones (Chapter 5).

The test supplies we use are: _____

The supplies are kept: _____

Please record the results of any blood or urine tests in the log book.

Time: _____ Result: _____

🐾 Side Trips

Please be sure that if the child is away from home, with you or with friends, extra snacks and a source of sugar are taken along.

🐾 Other Concerns
Concerns that we have are:

_____

_____

_____

_____

_____

_____

If there are any questions or if our child does not feel good or vomits, please call us or the other people listed above.

Thank you.

Be prepared for anything when you're planning to camp or vacation.

Chapter 25

VACATIONS AND CAMP

Special planning is important for vacations.

WHEN TRAVELING WHAT SHOULD PLANNING INCLUDE?

- Insulin, blood sugar test strips, and glucagon must be kept in a plastic bag in a cooler if traveling by car. All three will spoil if they get above 90° F or if they freeze.

- If the meter has been in a cold place, it should be brought to room temperature before doing a blood sugar test.

- Car travel may result in higher blood sugars due to less activity. Extra insulin is sometimes given.

- Remember to take supplies for measuring ketones.

- Supplies should be carried on airplanes and not left in luggage.

- Since 9/11/01, it is important with airplane travel to have a vial of insulin with a pre-printed label on the outside of the box. The glucagon should also be left in its original container. There have been no problems with taking insulin, insulin pumps or other diabetes supplies through x-ray security.

- Extras of everything should be carried by a second person on the plane when possible, in case one carry-on is lost.

- Extra snacks should be carried in case food is late or not available.

- Time changes within the U.S. are usually not a problem, but they must be considered if going overseas (call your doctor). For insulin pumps, the time in the pump is just reset.

- If activity is to be increased (playing at the beach, fishing, hiking, going to an amusement park, etc.), the insulin dose should be decreased.

CAMP

- Diabetes camp is often the first chance for a child and parents to show they can survive without each other. Most camps have doctors and nurses present so that the children are safe. Getting to know other children with diabetes who are of a similar age can be very helpful. Most of all, camp should be fun!

- If going to a non-diabetes camp (or school camp/outdoor lab):

    • It is essential the camp nurse and cabin counselor know about diabetes (low blood sugars and what to do, high blood sugars and what to do, illness and what to do, etc.).

    • Insulin changes for camp will need to be made by the child's diabetes doctor or nurse.

    • *All* diabetes supplies will need to be provided by the family.

    • Phone numbers need to be provided to report blood sugars and receive insulin dose changes and for any emergency.

Swimming is fun . . .

...and so is riding a horse.

Using an insulin pump sometimes increases
one's energy.

Chapter 26 USE OF INSULIN PUMPS IN DIABETES MANAGEMENT

THE PUMP

The insulin pump is a microcomputer (the size of a pager) which delivers insulin in a pattern more like the normal pancreas. Pumps have become more popular in recent years. *Only short-acting insulin is used in pumps.*

HOW IS INSULIN GIVEN BY THE PUMP?

- The **basal** dose delivers a preset amount of insulin each hour.

- A **bolus** dose is programmed by the person wearing the pump (or by an adult) each time food is eaten or if a high blood sugar is found.

WHAT IS INVOLVED WHEN STARTING ON A PUMP?

• The pump is more work than shots, not less. The first week (and for some, the first month) is the most difficult.

• At least four blood sugar tests must be done each day.

• Carbohydrate counting (see Chapter 12) and correction factors (Chapter 21) are usually used to determine bolus doses.

• When young children are treated with a pump, the parents are generally responsible for counting carbohydrates and giving the bolus insulin doses.

• Basal and bolus insulin doses are individualized for each person.

• Close contact with the health care providers is essential.

• Our experience shows that children do well if they and their parents are both highly motivated.

• *The person with diabetes must be ready for the pump.* It must not be just the parents!

THREE MAIN PROBLEMS SEEN WITH INSULIN "PUMPERS":

1. forgetting to give bolus doses

2. getting lazy and not doing at least four blood sugar tests per day

3. the cannula (tube) coming out from under the skin and blood sugars (± ketones) rapidly rising (remember: only short-acting insulin is used in a pump)

When a family is ready to consider use of an insulin pump, Chapter 26 in the larger book should be read. They should then discuss the possibility with their diabetes care providers.

The person with diabetes must want to use the pump (<u>NOT</u> just the parents).

FOOD IN MOUTH, HAND ON PUMP!

Good sugar control prior to pregnancy is
essential!

Chapter 27

PREGNANCY AND DIABETES

Pregnancy is possible for women with diabetes who do not have severe problems with complications.

WHAT IS IMPORTANT WHEN THINKING ABOUT GETTING PREGNANT?

🐾 Pregnancy should be <u>planned</u>.

🐾 The best blood sugar control possible should be achieved before and during pregnancy. The HbA_{1c} should be below 7.2% (or preferably 6.5%).

🐾 The risk of a miscarriage as well as birth defects in the baby are less if blood sugars are normal or near normal when the pregnancy begins.

HOW CAN THE BEST BLOOD SUGAR CONTROL BE DONE?

🐾 Intensive insulin therapy is usual during pregnancy. This includes:

- an insulin pump or frequent insulin shots

- frequent blood sugar checks (six to seven a day)

- paying close attention to nutrition

- frequent contact with the health care team

🐾 The target values for blood sugars are lower than usual and are given in the table in *Understanding Diabetes*.

🐾 Clinic visits are also more often: usually every two to four weeks.

WHAT ABOUT COMPLICATIONS AND PREGNANCY?

 Kidney damage is not a problem during pregnancy unless already present before the pregnancy. Medicines used to prevent kidney damage called "ACE-inhibitors" should not be taken during pregnancy. This medicine could cause birth defects in the baby.

 The eyes should be checked more often during pregnancy (at least every three months). If moderate damage is already present, this may get worse during pregnancy.

 Gestational diabetes is diabetes which occurs as a result of the stress of the pregnancy.

• After diagnosis, the care is like the care of a person who had diabetes prior to pregnancy.

• It usually goes away after pregnancy. There is an increased risk of developing diabetes later in life.

Chapter 28

RESEARCH AND TYPE 1 DIABETES

This area is always changing.

THE FOUR SUBJECTS PEOPLE ASK MOST ABOUT ARE:

❶ A cure: Pancreas or islet transplantation is already possible. The problem is that the strong medicines necessary to prevent rejection can be more harmful than having diabetes. Many new medicines are being tried, but it is still early. Fortunately, advances are being made in the intensive management of diabetes, providing this as an option to surgical transplantation and a life of immunosuppression.

❷ Non- or minimally invasive glucose monitoring (not having to poke a finger for every sugar level):

Two devices have been approved:

A. The Continuous Glucose Monitoring System® (CGMS) from Medtronic/MiniMed:

• The CGMS requires a cannula (tube) to be inserted under the skin.

• It gives sugar levels every five minutes for up to 72 hours. A sample tracing is in Chapter 28 of _Understanding Diabetes_.

• Blood sugars cannot yet be read as they are done ("real-time") but only by putting the device into a downloading dock connected to a computer.

• Four finger poke blood sugars must be done each day while wearing the CGMS and entered into the monitor.

B. The GlucoWatch® G2™ Biographer from Cygnus:

• The GlucoWatch pulls fluid from under the skin using a small current from an AAA battery in the watch.

• A two-hour warm-up time is needed initially.

• A finger-poke blood sugar is then done and entered into the watch for calibration.

• A glucose level, which can be read on the watch, is determined every 10 minutes for up to 13 hours.

- It has a high and a low sugar alarm and an alarm for a rapidly falling sugar level.

- Red marks may be left on the skin either under the pad or from the adhesive material around the watch.

- If the watch is removed leaving the sensor on the skin, a bit of Unisolve™ applied around the sensor edges will help to prevent the outer red marks (to keep from tearing the skin as the sensor is removed).

🐾 Prevention of type 1 diabetes:

- The first two large clinical trials began in the 1990s.

- In the U.S., people can call 1-800-425-8361 to find out where to go for a free TrialNet antibody screening. This area is moving very rapidly.

- Three biochemical islet cell antibodies (Chapter 3) are being used to determine if the autoimmune process has begun.

- Prevention trials are now focused on:

~ preventing the autoimmune process from starting

~ reversing the antibodies

~ stopping further damage after diabetes has been diagnosed

- It is likely that prevention will come before a safe cure.

🐾 Prevention of type 2 diabetes:

- This has already been shown to be possible.

- It involves eating less, exercising more and losing weight.

- It is discussed in Chapter 4 of _Understanding Diabetes_.

🐾 Prevention of complications:

- Diabetes complications of the eye and kidney are decreasing through attention being paid to the following:

~ better sugar control

~ blood pressure control

~ not smoking

~ yearly eye exams and urine microalbumin tests are essential after three years of diabetes in people age 12 years or older (see Chapter 22)

~ families may need to help remind their diabetes care provider to make sure these tests are done

110

Continuous Glucose Monitoring is coming!

Someday there will be a cure for diabetes!

PUBLICATIONS

The following publications and video may be purchased from The Guild of the Children's Diabetes Foundation at Denver (all orders must be pre-paid by credit card or check).

Understanding Diabetes this book covers all aspects of diabetes concerns. It is written at a level easily understandable to young adolescents and their families.

A First Book for Understanding Diabetes, a simplified book, in English or Spanish, for understanding diabetes.

Managing and Preventing Diabetic Hypoglycemia: A Video, this video is directed towards people of all ages and backgrounds offering suggestions on prevention and treatment of diabetic hypoglycemia.

For current prices and additional information, please call: **(303)863-1200 or (800)695-2873** or visit our website at: www.ChildrensDiabetesFdn.org

Make checks payable to:
The Guild-CDF at Denver

Mailing address:
The Guild of the
Children's Diabetes Foundation
777 Grant Street
Suite 302
Denver, CO 80203

All orders must be paid in full before delivery with a check or major credit card. Allow one to three weeks for delivery.

Canadian and Foreign Purchasers: Please include sufficient funds to equal U.S. currency exchange rates.